FREEDOM AND FAITH

FREEDOM AND FAITH

The Impact of Law on Religious Liberty

edited by

Lynn R. Buzzard

CROSSWAY BOOKS ● WESTCHESTER, ILLINOIS
A DIVISION OF GOOD NEWS PUBLISHERS

142709

Freedom and Faith: The Impact of Law on Religious Liberty copyright © 1982 by the Christian Legal Society. Published by Crossway Books, a division of Good News Publishers, Westchester, Illinois 60153.

First printing, 1982

Printed in the United States of America.

Library of Congress Catalog Card Number 81-71345

ISBN 0-89107-230-6

CONTENTS

PREFACE

Lynn R. Buzzard

Law and politics are uncomfortable and largely unfamiliar terrain for the church and for people of piety. Yet it is in such surroundings that significant struggles are now being carried out which affect both the life of the church and the rights of the individual believer. The struggles will likely also shape the character of the public order and the role of religious life and conscience in that public arena for decades, if not centuries.

Recent events in Poland dramatically illustrate how basic rights of the church and individuals can be swept aside by the power of the state. For Solidarity, for breadwinners, and for worshippers in Poland, it is clear that the quality of human life is vitally related to issues of law, politics, and the uses of power.

This volume is a collection of essays delivered at a conference conducted by the Christian Legal Society which addressed the issue of the impact of law and government policy on religious freedom. Such issues may seem unrelated to the many crises facing the world today. Yet the essays in this book deal precisely with issues of human value, the powers of government, the rights of conscience, and the character of public life. The source and character of law, the protection given human rights, the preservation of constitutional rights—these are at the heart of mankind's struggle for a way through the twenty-first century. The Christian Legal Society shares with many the conviction that, however vital religious life may presently be in our society, there are fundamental shifts in our culture and in our law which threaten the vital rights of religious liberty guaranteed by the Free Exercise Clause of the Constitution. Such rights must be vigorously preserved against the challenges of "public policy," "compelling state interest," and the secularism of our society.

It is our hope that these essays provide a perspective from which to view these emerging issues as well as a challenge to awareness and vigilance.

Lynn R. Buzzard
Executive Director
Christian Legal Society

FOREWORD
Julius B. Poppinga

The Christian community is at the point of competing and converging currents. One threatens us, the other invites us, and between the two we are buffeted about. The threatening current is Orwell's 1984, focusing to some degree upon the Christian community. At times we feel the courts, the Internal Revenue Service, the state securities bureaus, the county boards of taxation, and municipal zoning authorities are all casting a cynical and scrutinizing eye on evangelical outreach, whether it is a church, an agency of the church, a mission body, publishing house, school, or an ad hoc ministry. I think we sense this pressure, and we have to learn how to react to this pressure, how to deal with it, and how to conduct our affairs in a way which does not bring upon us unnecessary government intrusion and scrutiny. We also must take care to do what we do honestly in the sight of all men so that the name of Christ is not dishonored.

The other current is one that gives us great encouragement and hope. I believe that at no time, except perhaps in the earliest decades of this nation's history, has the evangelical Christian community enjoyed such visibility. I hesitate to use the term "enjoy." I'm not sure it is the appropriate term. But the presence of the body of Christ in our society today is of greater potential influence than has been the case for many years.

Results of a survey conducted by the Connecticut Mutual Life Insurance Company reflect a finding which those who conducted it did not expect and did not intend. It revealed a focus on religious faith as the one factor that most consistently and dramatically affects the values and behavior of the American people. That may come as a surprise to us, perhaps because we are in the habit of focusing on the negative. John C. Pollack, director of that study, reports the influence of religion "has penetrated virtually every dimension of American experience. It is a stronger determinant of our values than any other factor, liberal or conservative, old or young, white or black, male or female, rich or poor. The findings suggest that the increasing impact of religion on our social and political institutions may be only the beginning of a trend that could change the face of America."

Now those would be rather pretentious words if they were my own or if they had come from any single observer. The fact that they reflect the findings of a neutral study, not intended to yield that kind of result, is significant.

Mr. Pollack concludes his report: "Moral issues through religion have vaulted to the forefront of the political dialogue. Something unusual is happening." Indeed something unusual *is* happening, and we can be a unique part of it.

1 AMERICA TODAY: SHAKING FOUNDATIONS

Lynn Buzzard

Law in a Trembling Culture

Daniel Yankelovich, commenting on the changes taking place in contemporary American culture, writes, "A recurring image comes to mind—the image of the earth, moving deep beneath the surface and so transforming the landscape that it loses its comfortable familiarity . . . (the) giant plates of American culture are shifting relentlessly beneath us." Yankelovich's vision of a cultural upheaval sending tremors throughout our sociological and psychological body is reinforced by the title of his book *New Rules: Searching For Self-Fulfillment in a World Turned Upside Down,* in which he seeks to interpret collected data about the values of our society. He concludes, "We are not going back to the old values," but rather we are in the midst of an irresistible cultural revolution which constitutes a "decisive break" with the past. It is, he insists, drawing on an image of Hannah Arendt, the creation of a "new story."

The author's image is a powerful and accurate one.

There is a straining of the plates, a shaking of the foundations. The coalescing of economic uncertainty, the emergence of pluralistic and competing values, the rejection of old traditions and structures, the ecological plight of planet earth, the awareness through instant communications of the world's tragedies, the failure of the hopes and little gods of both Western and Eastern culture, the impotence of flower children and social reformers—are but a few of the factors causing us to feel that the grounds upon which we have built our ethos are shifting and shaking. Nor has the retreat from the world into self-fulfillment, self-empowerment and narcissistic searches for identity brought relief. So broad and acknowledged is this crisis that *Time* devotes an issue to the recovery of "spirit" and a portion of its publications to instances of "spirit" in the world. Artists have known of the crisis, and novelists like Kesey and Camus have sketched its dimensions with painful power. Even if we've missed its sometimes subtle presence in the arts, we all have known it with devastating reality in the lives of our friends.

If the "new story" image adopted by Yankelovich is accurate, it is not clear whether the story is comedy or tragedy, what the plot is or even who its main characters are. The most striking aspect of the situation in which we find ourselves is that when one reads the worldly philosophers, neither do they know. Perhaps it is because the landmarks are gone. We must chart the tremors, primarily in the legal, and more specifically, constitutional landscape. We must in that context ask difficult questions about the role of law in a pluralistic society, about where law will find its jurisprudential root in an ethos enamored all too often with positivism, about the relation of law to social policy and social policy to values and values to morality and morality to religion, about law's relationship to freedom as enabler and limiter. We must consider law's relationship to community as encoder and sustainer. Consider law and conscience and rebellion, and issues as old as law and faith.

While we may at times seem preoccupied with a legal argument here or a court citation there, it is clear that the situation in which we find ourselves shakes to the surface issues rarely observed because they usually lie so deep in our philosophic foundation. Now they have thrust themselves like giant faults onto the surface. These issues are the stuff out of which briefs, memoranda and arguments are made. Behind *Yoder* v. *Wisconsin,* behind *Schempp,* behind *Roe* v. *Wade* are the greater issues of community, ultimate values, perspectives on human life, culture, freedom and individual rights. To pretend they are simply about statutory construction, *stare decisis* and intent of the framers is to further cloud the scope of society's travail. They are, in fact, questions about jurisprudence and jurisprudence is about right and truth, and those are about religion.

Though law by no means is the occasion of our crises, nor the sole manifestation of it, it is a discipline and arena which naturally absorbs many of the tremors of our cultural *angst.* Like religion, it is a discipline that lives on the fault lines of our culture and also, it is a discipline uniquely helpless without foundations, without roots. If Hannah Arendt is correct, that the crisis of our age is one of authority, then law especially is in crisis. Law carries within its codes and precedents the weight of a culture, the accumulated wisdom (as well as prejudice and privilege) of a society. When that society trembles, when those values are assaulted, law is especially vulnerable. How much more so when law, having chosen to abandon itself to sociology, is without referent.

There is an irony in all this shaking and falling. It is precisely the collapse of so many "stories," to use Arendt's image, so many institutions and structures of society, the fading of visions and dreams turned illusion, that law by default has become so important. When extended families are disappearing and nuclear families are unstable, when community is tenuous and fragmented, when religion is too often impotent in the face of injustice and chaos, when human warmth wanes, there is a tendency to turn to law—to hope that law will preserve us. It is striking that in our day both the right and the left, the traditionalist and the innovator are increasingly conscious of the power of law and in particular the judiciary. And yet legal institutions are so helpless and vulnerable themselves in the face of the massive problems in our society. There is indeed no salvation in the law. The rush to law may tell us a lot about the lawlessness in the land. How are courts to provide principled leadership in the crises of our cities, in the bioethical issues surrounding us, in the task of creating a viable pluralistic society, of coordinating values and freedom, liberty and responsibility, law and morality? In the face of such issues, how tragic is the observation of a lawyer/theologian that "jurisprudence is deserted."

It is in the context of law's own crises of authority and identity and the increasing rejection of law by much of society, so that one author even spoke of the rule of law as an "obsolete faith," that the evangelical community has discovered the law and legal system. For too long Christians ignored law as a discipline too worldly and tainted for discipleship. As a result there was little development in the modern religious community of a theology of law, much less a commitment to participate in the framing of a legal strategy. The movement toward a more holistic theology and a growing sense of oppression have combined to thrust the religious community before the courts and into the legislatures. Such a development is healthy so long as law does not become our "refuge and strength." If the move to law expresses a concern for careful and just adjudication of rights and responsibilities within the framework of our cultural responsibility, and the insistence on preserving important liberties, then the presence of the Christian community in the courts can only be salutary. If, however, the move to law represents an attempt to "use" the law to avoid public responsibility or to "enforce" by code some value we have failed to adequately present in convincing fashion, or if law is an attempt to create a systemic resistance to broad liberty interests, then we shall have rendered a disservice to both law and faith.

What's Going On Here?

I would like to suggest that the current explosion of litigation in what is traditionally called the "church-state" area involves much more than the role of those two institutions. In fact, even framing the questions in such a fashion—that is, as "church-state" issues—confuses the character of the questions and, unfortunately, tends to result in sudden and inappropriate images of "high and impregnable walls of separation." A major element in this explosion of litigation is the vastly expanding role of government and a resultant shift in the way persons perceive their relationship to government. There is a loss of the sense of "us" about government and its related agencies, bureaucracies, standards and policies. "Law" is seen as a part of "them"—an alien force no longer the preserver of culture but the instrument of change. "Law" which within a few years shifts from declaring homosexual acts as criminal to being an instrument of guaranteeing that such conduct will not encounter "discrimination" creates confusion—and even anger—about its role. Law is no longer part of "our" comprehendable continuity.

The recent presidential election perhaps reflected an increasing mood that government is part of "them," not part of "us." This mood emerges in part from human tendencies to resist authority and find an enemy, but it has even more foreboding sources. The seemingly inexorable tendency of government to expand the sphere of its dominance has, I believe, contributed heavily to this alienation.

Government, and its often-allied cousin, law, invade our lives. They control our businesses, our schools, our states. They assess, demand, codify—they regulate, certify, license—they tax, they aid, they insure. This expansiveness combined with an audacious claim to "right" and authority is an offense to the strong element of freedom in the American experience dating to the casting off of the yoke of British colonialism. The currently mild resurgence of libertarianism is but another expression of this sense that government consists inordinately of controllers, each with a messianic vision, each with a religious zeal to do his own version of justice backed by a bible of regulatory powers. Even for those who may affirm the necessity of strong government to counterbalance potentially destructive forces in other segments of our society or to deal with world and national problems beyond the scope of self-reliant individualism, there is a growing concern about the power of those who insist on doing us "good."

An expansive government leads to litigation over individual rights, freedom, balance of powers, due process and civil rights and tends as well to consume all the territory between the individual and the state—the area of associational life—those structures which are essential to community and to identity and which are loci of responsibility. They are the mediating structures of a culture. An expansive omnipresent state tends to monopolize the landscape—to convert by regulation such private associational life and philanthropy into an arm of the state.

Expansive Religion

Government is not the only factor in the current mix leading to confrontation. For just as government has been expanding, so has the religious arena. In the culture context this has taken place in two distinct ways, both of which are highly relevant to the litigation now facing the courts. One is the increasing involvement of organized

religion in public and institutional programs and ministries. Religion has become big business. Its economic
power is, at least cumulatively, massive, and its presence
ubiquitous. The Christian community has expanded
beyond the local church and church camps, even beyond
the occasional orphanage or hospital to very large enterprises, including education, social welfare, child care, shel-
tered workshops, broadcasting, programs for senior
citizens, day camps, food banks, relief ministries, child
placement services, counseling programs, medical clinics
and even a few legal services for the poor. The sheer scope
of these enterprises, the dollars involved and the institutional machinery created to enable and protect them are
evidence that government is not the only "growth indus-
try" in our social fabric. This commentary is not a critique
of this broad participation in our culture; in fact, it is essential to the character of a Christian community which rightly understands its relationship to culture, to justice and to
human need. I am suggesting that an expansive religion
inevitably leads to contact, tension and an occasional clash
with other nonreligious groups engaged in similar charitable efforts, even more tense collisions with private prof-
it-oriented enterprises engaged in such activities and certainly with the involvement directly or by regulation of
government. The overlapping zones of interest, even
without a clash of fundamental values, creates potential for
sustaining more than a few legal firms in the years ahead.

The second aspect of expanding religion is not so much
about the scope of religion's involvement, but the diverse
character of religion itself. At least we used to know what
religion was. It was Protestants, Catholics, and Jews with
the addition of a few strange groups which were tolerated
as quaint symbols of our diversity. At least we all pretty
much shared a Judeo-Christian perspective. Today however it is not at all clear what is even "religion." The
emergence of highly visible, though numerically small,

bands of believers, of Eastern religions, of basketball play-
ers with Islamic names, of mail order ordinations, of com-
munes and cities claiming tax exemptions have raised new
social and legal questions about what is religion. And what
of sincerely held beliefs not rooted in theism? One is in-
clined to plead for the real religion to please stand up. For a
society which offers great freedoms and considerable privileges to religious-based beliefs, the range of religious expression in our society has posed serious problems—problems which in law get framed as issues of equal protection
and establishment, but which mirror a larger question:
What forms of belief and action does society wish to protect, enable and/or excuse from otherwise applicable regulations?

Expansive Secularism
Still another expansive force is a major factor in the litigation environment, and contributes tensions within our culture. This third force is ideological and therefore perhaps
systemic and more difficult to identify and challenge. Its
cultural imperialism is more aggressive and, from my
perspective, more dangerous. Secularism, or "secular humanism," has emerged as a dominant perspective of much
of contemporary culture.

Literature attacking secular humanism has often ex-
aggerated its cohesiveness as a philosophy, and has granted
it credit for much more than it deserves. When, however,
appropriate limits have been placed upon the critique, it is
accurate to say that there is a systematic attempt to assert
secular humanistic values as operative assumptions in
much of our cultural life, especially in the educational
arena.

We must carefully distinguish this secularistic philosophy from pluralism. Pluralism may indeed be threatening
or offensive to some persons, but if we are to take seriously freedom and human rights, pluralism must not be only
grudgingly accepted, but affirmed. In fact there are posi-

tive aspects to pluralism for the religious community—it is, after all, the essential context for evangelism and prose-lytism, it invites the religious community to take seriously its apologetic tasks. It forces serious decision-making about commitments in life. It requires the church to really be the church and the believer to really be the believer. It forces choices. Christians did quite well, after all, in the pluralism of the first century. And we might as well face up to pluralism now. To those who thought pluralism meant Catholics and Jews, ethnic foods and regional accents, there is a psychic shock. The varieties of groups inviting our allegiance (and contributions) is liable to disturb those accustomed to a cultural consensus. Gays are not the only ones who have come out of their closets to assert their rights to participate in our social, economic and political life. *Playboy* and *Penthouse* take their place beside *Fortune* and *Time* at the corner drugstore.

While affirming pluralism, there is a so-called pluralism which is unacceptable, and that is one which degenerates into a religion of secularism, excluding religion from participation in the pluralism. It is a pluralism which encourages expression of all viewpoints and values EXCEPT those which emerge from a religious commitment. It has been the perspective of the Center for Law and Religious Freedom that a secularism which masquerades as pluralism is not constitutionally mandated, and is constitutionally proscribed as a denial of equal protection.

That tendency is perceived in extreme views of "separation" of church and state so that one sees U.S. district courts holding that universities, those places committed to free expression and student rights, those marketplaces of ideas, may not permit religious students to have the same rights to meet and discuss their ideas that other students have. One court put it bluntly when it declared that religious speech is not entitled to the same protection as political speech.

It is beyond the scope of this paper to explore the

character and impact of secularism as a philosophy essentially hostile to the religious assertions regarding truth, values and human nature. But it seems unchallenged that the principles enunciated in the Humanist Manifesto are fundamentally alien to the commitments of the Christian community and virtually any religious body. It is perhaps a sign of the times that the equal protection clause of the Constitution is being used increasingly by the religious community to assert rights enjoyed by competing secular philosophies.

The Task Before the Religious Community: A Prophetic Perspective

In the context of a virulent secularism and expansive state, what is the task of the religious community in general and, more specifically, of the Christian community? Where shall the Christian community stand when the foundations are shaking, when all of us are, in Camus' image, infected with the plague?

For such a time as this was made the prophetic tradition. In the biblical story, the prophet played a special role in times of cultural crisis, of struggles over identity, purpose and mission. The prophet came in those moments when Israel asked, "Is there any word from God?" Prophets came when communities of faith seemed overwhelmed, when institutions were collapsing, when symbols of religion were excised or had become idolatrous. It was precisely in such contexts that prophets spoke words—rarely words of superficial comfort, but life-giving. They were words of history, of judgment, or repentance, of covenant and community. It is perhaps time for a prophet and prophet's perspective.

It is sobering to remember that the prophets were more admired by history than by their contemporaries. There is something in the very character of times which called forth prophets that they were rarely heard. They did not build structures and institutions which challenge EEOC regulations or develop complex legal charters to minimize government regulation and insure their 501 (c) (3) status. They had no great prophetic crusades, tape ministries, TV networks—not so much because they would have declined to use such devices as that no one would support them. They never had to ponder the issue of whether to use blue envelopes or green ones for a business reply envelope. Thus when one pleads for a prophet, one might be asking for a word one doesn't want to hear, but surely nothing less is worth hearing.

A second caveat to the plea for a prophet is to remember that within the biblical tradition there were a host of prophets, even prophet bands, and most were unfaithful, false and political soothsayers. They were the culturally seduced, the fair-haired boys of the establishment, the assurers of victory. There will always be many who will say that they are the awaited prophet and it will take a great deal of wisdom to distinguish the true from the false. And certainly the test cannot be mere religiousness or success.

But with those warnings, we must still plead for the prophet. There are three perspectives of prophets in particular which may significantly inform the response of the believing community to the situation in which we find ourselves. They are a historic, even cosmic perspective, a serving remnant as the instrumentality of God's redemption, and a commitment to justice as the mark of God's character and that of the remnant community.

A Historic Perspective

Nothing emerges more clearly from an examination of Old and New Testament biblical traditions than the conviction that God is a God of history. He is perceived precisely through the stuff of history—a salvation history made up of kings, wars, slave rights and turf. No escape to "religion" in this commitment. It is out of the raw history of Abraham, Isaac and Jacob and places like Bethel and Bethlehem that the faith is born and nurtured. In this sense Christianity is the least "spiritual" of all religions, its heart quickening not so much to ideas or mystical experience as to people streaming out of Egypt and to crucifixions. History is the arena of revelation and the locus of discipleship. The faith is not so much an escape from the vicissitudes of life as an engagement in them. The prophets thus speak not only of spiritual idolatry but of social injustice, of military alliances, and commercial justice at the gate.

With this prophetic perspective, the religious community which shapes its life around these commitments will hear nothing of "sticking to religion." In fact it is precisely "sticking to religion" in the narrow sense of rituals and doctrines that caused the prophet to declare that such acts had become a stench in the nostrils of a God who demanded justice and righteousness in all aspects of a nation's life. The Christian will seek to manifest righteousness in every arena of life and to look to the mundane, worldly and earthly for manifestations of judgment and grace. Charles Malik recently complained that too much of evangelicalism knows only three realities: the self, the Bible and Christ, but knows nothing of history and culture and human thought. To preach salvation is, to be sure, to speak of the individual's capacity to be born from above and experience the fullness of Christ's forgiveness and the indwelling of the Spirit, but it is also to recognize the plea in Romans and the promise in Ephesians that all creation come to acknowledge God and find its unity in Him. The salvation of the individual is but a part of God's full intent to exercise His Lordship over all creation. This is one point on which both the Sojourners and the Christian Political Action Movement agree. The Christian insists that God has not abandoned His original intent and moved to plan "B." His promise is that He shall in the fullness of time manifest that Lordship.

"Lordship" is perhaps the most comprehensive and revolutionary statement of the gospel. The term is not, as so often seems the case in religious prayer and conversation, a term of endearment or a synonym for "sweet" or "kind." In the New Testament it is the Greek "*kyrios*" which is cognate to "caesar," "kaiser" and "czar"—none of whom were noted for sweetness. They were noted for power and authority. It is the declaration of the ultimate authority of Christ. Ephesian Christians in the Roman Empire did not court hostility because they thought Jesus was "sweet" or because they thought they would go to heaven when they died. They did not anger Romans or worshippers of Diana because they thought the teachings of Jesus were good advice. What Rome could not tolerate was the belief by Ephesian Christians that Jesus was *kyrios*—Lord, and that was a direct assault on the Roman assertion of final authority.

The practical consequence of believing that Christ is Lord of all is that the Christian community will resist the attempt to confine its activities to what the secularist defines as "religion." Politics, art, science and philosophy all comprise the arena of activity for the believing community. The criticism of religious groups on the "right" based on their involvement in politics is particularly ill conceived. One may debate their choice of issues or even the side they take on some, but no one within the biblical tradition dares challenge their assertion that as believers they are compelled to speak to the moral character and the political life of the nation. The involvement in politics will, of course, not be motivated simply by a design to "protect" Christians or evangelize the political world (narrowly speaking), but to address the very core issues of political/public/social life.

Those informed by the prophetic tradition will not be satisfied with being "left alone." They will seek a structure which allows dialogue, engagement, judgment and restoration. Free exercise will not be construed as merely creating a zone of non-governmental interference or the creation of an exemption from conscience-opposed activity, but the opportunity to be full partners in the pluralism of our day. The believer will not, of course, always be politically successful, and must be sensitive to the rights of others, eager to preserve wide zones of freedom for all persons.

Related to this commitment to history is a commitment to the role of community and culture in shaping life. In the Old Testament in particular there is the clear recognition that not just individuals but "nations" have a personality and character. The concept of covenant and community, even the role of law in that community, gives evidence of the biblical commitment to culture. Culture is expressive or resistive to covenant living. And quite clearly community and culture are broader than religion, narrowly conceived. They include civil law and government which are gifts of God. It is not only "religion" which gives a gift to culture, but government as well. The believer will thus be concerned to assist in a crucial dialogue about the relationship of community values and traditions versus the rights of individuals. This will surely raise complex issues such as those in the classic Hart-Devlin debates, but it is an essential conversation. Christians should be joining those who raise serious sociological and psychological questions about the American enamoration with individualism, often at the cost of community. How to relate the sustenance of community values, and a culture's values and traditions, how to avoid losing one's roots without overwhelming important liberties of individuals and minority groups are difficult issues, and profoundly pressing ones.

I am reminded of the biological concept of territoriality, referring to the habits of some animals in staking out a piece of turf, a territory which is "theirs." Conflicts emerge when there is an invasion of another's "territory."

There is a sense in which the concept of territoriality is used by some to suggest that religionists ought to "stay in their place." Such persons offer the religious person a certain "territory"—usually including prayers, worship services, Bibles, gospel singing and, of course, everything after we die. Too many Christians have accepted that offer, stayed in their "place" and accepted the exclusion of religion from art, science, philosophy and education. Such a restriction must be vigorously rejected as contrary not only to our understanding of the scope of our faith commitment, but contrary to that which gives health and vitality to a civilization. Surely in the crises of our culture, it is a loss to exclude from the nurturing and sustaining elements, the insights and gift of faith. Rather than seeking to exclude from all public presence the strengths of religious communities and faith, our culture ought to be encouraging the participation in public life of all who come with values and commitments.

This perspective on the significance of the historical process in God's story gives to the believing community a special task to develop an adequate philosophy of history, culture and the place of government in God's order. No legal strategy for First Amendment liberties, no arguments for Free Exercise, no attempt to preserve the spiritual values of our heritage dares ignore this prior task. Only through such creative work can we correctly apply the truth of Christ's reign over creation—and history. We must never baptize "what is" with God's will. This attempts to displace Him from history and denies His authority over humanity.

A Servant Remnant

The second critical element of a prophetic tradition which can speak to our situation is the emphasis on the believing community as a remnant with the style of a servant—to be blessed and to be a blessing as with the Abrahamic covenant. This theme is especially prominent in those contexts in which the community of Israel is subject to the power of a larger and hostile political force. This image and understanding of the role of the believing community in a pluralistic or hostile environment may be instructive for our present situation and may also assist in avoiding some of the potentially dangerous versions of the concept of Lordship over all history and creation. One such tendency is to use that theology to impose a theocratic state or to attempt to use political power to establish a state which conforms to the religious images. No tyrant is quite so fearful as one with a theocratic theology.

The prophetic imagery of Israel as a suffering servant and remnant people suggests a number of themes appropriate to our situation. First, it suggests that the people of God are a minority people. This may seem in striking emotional contrast to the imagery of Yahweh as the Lord of history and creation, and implies that His Lordship is not now manifest. It is the hope and eschatological vision of Israel, but it is not now reality. What is reality is that the people of God are a remnant, a minority people. No admission is perhaps more painful to contemporary Christians in America than that. It is an acknowledgment of our cultural and evangelistic failure. It is an attack on psyche. Our American culture makes it especially painful because we are used to being winners. Being *numero uno* is part of our American self-assessment. We are the nation that wins its wars and beats the Russian hockey team. We must be best. First in space, first on the moon. We are the nation of the Yankees, Coca Cola, and IBM. The biggest and the best.

Suffering, losing, being second best is alien to our psychology. It is expressed in the oft-quoted phrase, "winning isn't the most important thing, it is the only thing." We haven't learned much about captivity, much less how to thrive in captivity. That may explain part of our deep frustration in American society today at seeing the culture move away from religious symbolism and institutional support for our values and norms. We in the mainstream of American Protestantism or even the mainstream of evangelicalism are used to having institutional support, at least informal support. After all, our country was formed for freedom of worship, nursed in prayer, schooled on the Scriptures. It is the land of thanksgiving proclamations and religious inscriptions on currency. In our better moments we knew all that verbiage was not identical to abiding faith and righteousness, but it was a comfortable environment for at least mainstream moderate faith. In addition to a more vigorous interaction with other value systems we better prepare those inner resources which are necessary to sustain vital and energetic spiritual life as a minority people.

Some groups believe our country's only moral and spiritual problems are a few bureaucrats, a couple of Supreme Court decisions, and a handful of gay rights ordinances—that if we could strip away these hostile accretions from the body politic we would get back to good old solid Christian America. I am not sure that is an accurate picture, and certainly not one the prophetic tradition sees. I suspect that if we strip the culture of whatever we find most offensive to our religious values we would not find Christian America, but an essentially materialistic and hedonistic culture.

The task before us is the one addressed by the prophetic community—to develop in the believing community the capacity to sing a song in a strange land—and to make that song something other than a dirge. Through the centuries the Jewish community and many less popular Christian groups have had to learn to do this. Early Christians did quite well as a minority people with little support from institutional structures and, as far as I can tell, without one emperor prayer breakfast or national television program.

They lived as a minority people and maintained an exuberance and joy of spirit. They avoided, in the main, the dangers which accompany minorities—neurotic separationism, courting of persecution, world rejection, exclusive other-worldiness.

Strategies which rely on political or legal structures to sustain religious values are doomed to failure. If that had been sufficient we would not be where we are today, for Christianity enjoyed that throughout much of our nation's history. While it will be crucial in the days ahead to struggle in the political and legal arena, this new burst of sensitivity to legal and political action may be no substitute for the nurturing of the spirit. There is in the prophetic tradition no promise of effectiveness. At times, in fact, such as with the commissioning of Ezekiel, there is a prospect of ineffectiveness. The only promise is of God's presence and the criticalness of proclaiming His truth.

Related to this recognition of minority status is developing the capacity to say "NO"! Throughout world history the capacity of morally conscious people, and especially of remnant people, to say "NO" to destructive and usurpative authority has been significant. Except for those religious traditions in our own country which have long felt a minority status, saying "NO" was considered both impolite and unbiblical. After all, government was instituted by God and obedience to authority was part of our tradition. It was an easy theology too, because we were the authority. It also provides an easy escape from faithfulness and responsibility. I suspect that as believers sense increased tension between their faith commitments and the values of a secular culture, they will increasingly feel the pressure and issue a gentle but firm "NO" to the expectations of culture, government, education and the shapers of our values be they NEA, political parties, ABA, AMA, TV magnates or whoever.

But when is it appropriate to resist? There is a spirit of militancy in some segments of the Christian community, but when is it appropriate? What demands go to the heart of faith? How does one say "no"? What is the appropriate role of government? What special treatment or exemption ought religion to expect from government as a right? As a privilege? For what will we go to the wall? These are urgent questions, the answers to which require a more carefully developed biblical concept of society and the state.

The final element of the servant-remnant-prophetic perspective is the emphasis on the "servant" role—a style which sees the faith community as existing not simply for its own self but to serve the nation, even the world, that the whole world may come to sense the love, justice and glory of God. And it will do this "not by might nor by power" but by the Spirit, through slain lambs, suffering servants, fishermen, little men in trees, weak things and little nations. The very election of Israel is a proclamation of the mystery of God's manner of witness, conversion and penetration. The Lord is indeed risen, but the rising followed obedience to death and a conscious rejection under temptation of the flamboyant, the economic and the political process. I am not convinced that this constitutes a rejection of involvement in such processes, but rather that the heart of the religious life is not entrenched in such structures and techniques. Again, in such a tradition free exercise is not a means of doing our own thing, but of freedom to serve, to risk, to die. It is a philosophy that runs, as one observer declared, "contrary to history." For those who work within and with institutions that represent power, influence and cultural dominance, that servant and suffering image must balance preoccupation with political coalitions, legislative strategies, demonstrations and media blitzes.

A God of Justice

There are many descriptions of God which are appropriate to our agenda. Certainly the prophetic image of a God of promise and hope is a powerful declaration to people who find themselves overwhelmed. The image of a God of judgment is both encouraging and frightening, the latter because that judgment is supremely addressed not to the hordes of the ungodly who do not know the Lord of history, but to those who are called.

Perhaps, however, no declaration needs to be heard more clearly than that God is a God of justice. Justice is a central proclamation of the prophetic tradition. It is God's name, His hope, His vision. To do justice is an act of worship. The biblical terms for righteousness and for justice come from the same root. For those of us with strong religious backgrounds, righteousness has been much demanded, much illustrated. But how few sermons on God's concern for justice—at the gate, for the poor and the oppressed. Our insistence on justice for the religious community will fall on deaf ears if we fail to show ourselves as a people with a commitment to justice for others. What do we more than the world if we only speak for justice when our own ox is gored? But if we speak for justice, work for justice, vote for justice, develop systems for justice, perhaps then, when we speak for our own cause, there will be a hearing. Our real commitment to justice will not be measured by whether we defend our own interests, but whether we defend those without the power or the means to raise their own defense. Perhaps we can begin to learn what it is like to feel the weight of a hostile culture, the pressure of opposition, and begin to respond to the cries of those far longer and more substantially pressured. If we feel occasionally the lack of justice in the context of our own freedoms, we may be more sensitive to the massive injustices which are often a part of the human condition.

Conclusion

What then is the response of the believing and prophetical-ly informed community in an unstable world? To again use Arendt's image of the "new story," it is to commit ourselves to be included in the writing of that story. If there is a new story being written, we must contribute to the development of its characters, plot and themes. Such a commitment comes not merely out of a concern for self-preservation or pious witness, but out of a commitment to our life together as bearing ultimate significance. This is not a legal game we are playing nor is it an academician's exercise in constitutional law, nor a historian's exploration of the forces that shaped the Constitution. We are talking about our people, our nation, our character, the values that shape us, the manner in which we shall develop our youth for responsible living, the way in which we identify and give strength to good and resist evil. It is about shaping life so it can survive psychologically and spiritually in the technological and potentially dehumanized world around us. This is no debate club exercise. This goes to the heart of both religion and society. The word is indeed to be made flesh and dwell among us. Like Christ we must weep over cities that refuse their destinies and like the rocks Paul describes in Romans, cry out for the redemp-tion of the world. It is not merely a historical interest in culture in the abstract. The tragedies that confront our modern world, the suffering of those living on the fault lines of our trembling culture are not simply statistics. We all can give names to the broken families, the meaningless and aimless lives, the violence, the hunger, the death, the victims of drugs, the vacant faces, the prisoners, the insti-tutionalized victims of a mechanistic and hedonistic spirit in our age. Is this really an age that can afford a high and impregnable wall interpreted as excluding, from public education, for example, any religiously derived values?

The commitment to help write the "story" that will shape lives must be comprised of salvation, wholeness, peace, justice, righteousness, love, covenant, liberty and freedom. Those themes are precisely what we are about. Have we not been asking our historians, our psychologists, our psychiatrists, our sociologists, our anthropologists, our politicians to give us more than bread—to give us purpose, hope, values, a vision—to help us find ourselves, to help us commit ourselves to human rights and justice, to sensitivity and caring, to expelling human prejudice, to combatting crime and delinquency? Then let us share in that talk as well, not as monopolists, theocrats, moral guardians, religious tyrants—but as fellow-citizens—and not as a people with an exclusive claim on the truth.

We are a part of this culture and shall insist on the climate of freedom and the power of religious liberty, not simply because we want to keep alive the quaint or bizarre, as one collects antiques, but because the world needs us. It needs desperately the call to sacrifice, the call to covenant, the call to justice and mercy, the call to righteousness. It needs articulate, activist, aggressive religion and communities of faith. We shall therefore resist attempts to use the predilections of Madison or the letters of Jefferson to exclude from the common discourse those values, visions and dreams which emerge from religion. We shall resist explicit or implicit attempts to exclude religion because it is divisive or controversial. Of course it is—so is Marxism, so is pornography, so is evolution, so is military spending. We dare not limit the field of discourse on the vital issues of our day to those who only hold their opinions mildly, to those who do not derive them from any ultimate commitments. In sum, we shall insist that the religious community intends to vigorously assert its civil rights.

We shall write this cultural story in a spirit of humility and the stance of a servant. We shall plead with our age not to sell its birthright for porridge, not to forget that man cannot live by bread alone. But we must not seek to use the sword where only the spirit can move. We shall seek to engage the world in creative and constructive ways, and even when we quarrel, to do so in the spirit which commends our Lord to the world. We shall remember that the mark of the faithful is not its cogency, its historical acuity or its legal sophistication, but its love.

2 HUMANISM VS. RELIGIOUS FREEDOM: A TIME TO ACT

Francis A. Schaeffer

The basic problem of Christians in the West in the last century in regard to society and the state is that they have seen things in bits and pieces instead of totals. They have very gradually become disturbed over permissiveness, pornography, the public schools, the breakdown of the family, and finally abortion. They have not, however, seen this as a whole. Each thing is a part, a symptom of a shift from the world view that was at least vaguely Christian in memory to a world view which is rooted in the concept that impersonal matter or energy, shaped into its present form by impersonal chance, is the final truth of what is. This is the total from which all these other things are only the symptoms.

These two world views stand as totals in absolute antithesis to each other, both in content and in results. This includes sociological and governmental results, and very specifically law. These two world views not only differ in content as to final reality. They inevitably produce totally different results.

Why have Christians been so slow to understand this? There are various reasons but the central one is a defective view of Christianity. Pietism was begun in Germany by P. J. Spener in the seventeenth century. It was a healthy thing in many ways in that it stood against pure formalism in religion and a too abstract concept of Christianity and theology. It had its poor side, however, in that it was platonic. It did not give sufficient place to the intellectual side of Christianity. Christianity and spirituality were shut up to a very small area of life. The totality of reality was neglected.

The poor side of Pietism and its resulting platonic outlook has been a tragedy. Rightly understood, true spirituality covers nothing less than the totality of life and reality.

Related to this is the fact that many Christians apparently do not mean what I mean when I say Christianity is true. They are Christians and they believe, for example, in the truth of creation, the truth of the virgin birth, of Christ's miracles, Christ's substitutionary death and His coming again, but they stop there. When I say that Christianity is true I mean it is true to the total reality—the total of what is—beginning with the central reality, the objective existence of the infinite personal God. To me the total reality shouts of the existence of the infinite personal God and then in various ways shouts of all that flows from that as it is given in the Bible (for example, creation, man made as unique in the image of God, the historic fall, redemption, and the final restoration).

The totality of reality necessitates the existence of the infinite personal God. To say it another way: there are no sufficient intellectual answers to the totality of reality except the Judeo-Christian answer. This concept may sound simple, but it is really quite revolutionary. Christianity is not a series of truths in the plural, but Truth. It is Truth about total reality, not just about religious things. Biblical

Christianity is truth concerning total reality and the intellectual holding of that total, and then, in some poor way, living in the light of that truth, which brings forth certain personal, governmental, and legal results.

In complete contrast, humanists who hold the materialistic final reality concept see final reality as material energy shaped by impersonal chance. It must be said to our shame that they saw the totalness of these two views, the Christian view and the humanist view, much sooner than the Christians. And then we must understand that, as the Christian view naturally brings forth certain personal conclusions but equally certain governmental and legal conclusions, so the humanist view brings forth certain results with inevitable certainty. Therefore, there are two total world views concerning reality and they inevitably bring forth certain results in all areas of life.

There is no way to mix these two total entities; it cannot be done. Liberal theology has been trying to do this from soon after the Enlightenment up to the present. And the liberal theologians, as naturally as a ship coming into port, have come down on the side of nonreligious humanism in regard to such things as life style, government, and law. Humanism, used in this way, means Man beginning from himself, with no knowledge or understanding outside of himself—Man being the measure of all things.

Nowhere have the results of these two total entities been more open to observation than in government and law. We take our form-freedom balance in government for granted. Some even regard it as natural. But it is not. No ancient culture produced it—certainly not the Greek city-states. Our form-freedom balance is a product of our Christian heritage, specifically that which grew up in Northern Europe following the Reformation.

The founding fathers of the United States understood these things in varying degrees. John Witherspoon was president of the College of New Jersey (now Princeton

University) and was a signer of the Declaration of Independence. He also had much input on various crucial committees in the founding of the country. He knew and stood consciously in the stream of thought that came forth from Samuel Rutherford's *Lex Rex; or the Law and the Prince.* Most people in this country no longer remember *Lex Rex.* But people like Witherspoon and others who founded America understood *Lex Rex* and what it represented—and they acted upon it.

People such as Thomas Jefferson, who was a Deist, may have known something of Samuel Rutherford's work. One man's philosophy these people certainly knew was that of John Locke. Examining Locke, it is clear that though he had secularized Rutherford's *Lex Rex,* he had drawn heavily from it.

The founding fathers knew very specifically and consciously what they were doing. In the Declaration of Independence they wrote about inalienable rights. Where do inalienable rights come from? Surely not from the government or the state, for then they could be taken away by the state. They founded the country upon the concept that there is Someone there, the Great Lawgiver, to give the rights. There was a paid chaplain functioning for the Continental Congress before the Revolutionary War was even finished. And the first Thanksgiving Day was called in order to say thank you to God when the war ended. These men really knew what they were doing, and they consciously understood the basis of the civil government which they had established. Moreover, we must remember that all the earlier provincial colonial legislatures opened with prayer. The founding fathers knew they were building on the concept of a Supreme Being who was the Creator, the final reality, and that without this what they were writing in the foundational documents of the country was nonsense.

It was not a vague concept of God but one which, even

for the Deists, was rooted in the Judeo-Christian memory.

Witherspoon's sermon on that first Thanksgiving Day shows this Christian perspective. He said: "A republic once equally poised must either preserve its virtue or lose its liberty." In an earlier speech Witherspoon said, "He is the best friend of American liberty who is most sincere and active in promoting pure and undefiled religion."

To have suggested to these men a viable state separated from religious influence would have utterly amazed them. The First Amendment was later added and had only two purposes: first, that there would be no established national church for the united thirteen states. Second, that the government would not interfere with the free practice of religion. These were the purposes of the First Amendment, and no other.

Another man who had a major impact on the thinking of the founders was William Blackstone. For him there were two foundations for law, nature and revelation. In his *Commentaries on the Law of England* he spelled out what he meant by revelation by speaking of "the divine law found only in the holy scripture." Until the takeover of the government and law in the United States by the humanistic world view, for a law student not to have mastered Blackstone's *Commentaries* would have meant that he would not have graduated from law school. That is how deeply Blackstone was rooted in American law until the relatively recent past. Now it is all gone.

We live in a secularized society with secularized, sociological law. Sociological law means that society does not function on any solid base of absolutes but only works upon that which a small group decides is for the sociological good of the people as a whole at that given moment. There have been various historical factors which have had an impact on the law in the United States. The basic reason for the change of law in this country, however, is the takeover by a humanist philosophy which could never have given the form and freedom which we have had in the United States. The form and freedom that we have had since the Reformation has rested upon a Christian base. And with humanism taking over and now becoming the consensus, this form and freedom is shaken to the core. We should not be at all surprised at what has happened because both the Christian world view and the naturalistic world view bring forth certain inevitable results, not only in personal lives but also in government and law.

In these shifts that have come in law, where have the Christian lawyers been? The shift has come gradually, but it has only come to its peak in the last forty or fifty years. Surely the Christian lawyers should have been the ones to have sounded the trumpet clear and loud. The nonlawyers like myself have a right to feel let down by the Christian lawyers. When I wrote *How Should We Then Live?* between 1974 and 1976 and was beginning to deal with the lordship of Christ and the whole of life in relationship to law and government, I found no writing explaining or clearly calling attention to the total shift in law and government. When I started researching and writing that book, I began from the point of secular philosophy, liberal theology, and the arts. Then I studied the courts, and especially the Supreme Court. I read Oliver Wendell Holmes and others. I was appalled at what these men were saying and by the rulings of the courts. It was exactly what I had been struggling with in modern secular philosophy and the other disciplines. In *How Should We Then Live?* I presented the abortion case as the clearest illustration of arbitrary, sociological law. The abortion case was the clearest illustration, but it was only the clearest illustration. The law in general has become relativistic. Law has become situational law, but of course this is the natural inevitable consequence of the materialistic concept of reality.

Presuppositions determine consequences. It is cause and effect. If one begins with the origin being the infinite personal God of the Judeo-Christian religion, then natural consequences or effects flow from that presupposition. These have effects on all areas of life including law and government. On the other hand, if one sees reality as only impersonal material or energy shaped only by impersonal chance, the natural conclusion is situational values, socio-logical law, and sociological government.

We are indeed way down the road toward a totally hu-manistic culture where law, and especially the courts, are being used as the vehicle to force this view and its results on the population. We are already a long, long way down the road.

In the face of this humanistic takeover Christians have been virtually silent. Liberal theology has contributed much to this silence. Liberal theology is only humanism using theological terms instead of philosophic terms. For a starting point, let us begin in 1893 with Dr. Charles A. Briggs. He was put out of the Presbyterian ministry be-cause of his teaching liberal, rationalistic theology. Then after that there was a great silence until the 1920s and 1930s. By then most of the old-line denominations had become dominated by liberalism at the two power centers, the bureaucracies and the seminaries. With rare excep-tions, when voices were raised it was too late. The Bible-believing theologians who saw the theological danger did not seem to understand that they were dealing with totals and not just bits and pieces. The theologians did not see the shift from one total world view to the other total world view in regard to culture and government.

To join the battle today with any intelligence we must understand that what we are facing is not just bits and pieces and not even just a question of religious truth. What is involved is the question of Truth in regard to total real-ity. To join the battle on the total front we must not even center the battle on freedom, and especially not just on *our* freedom. The battle must be centered on Truth—the truth of total reality. Biblical truth and humanism stand in total antithesis to one another.

We live in a democracy which was born out of a Christian base and which gives us freedom. However, such freedom is dwindling today. For example, a recent study states that out of 150 or so nations that exist in the world today, less than twenty-five have any real freedom. What we take for granted is exceedingly rare in the world today. We must use our freedom while we have it.

We must step out of a platonic concept of Christianity. We must emphasize as part of true spirituality the lordship of Christ; that is, Christ is Lord over the whole spectrum of life.

Unfortunately, a great deal of evangelical leadership has been shut up spiritually to a very narrow area of life. And it seems that very often the main concern is to preserve their own personal projects.

Evangelicals of our day seem to have forgotten the old revivals and what they have brought forth. It is true that the old revivals called for personal salvation. However, they also resulted in social action. Think of the Whitefield-Wesley revivals. Many historians say it was these revivals and the social changes which they brought which saved England from its own form of the French Revolution. The revivals in England and the United States called for social action as well as personal salvation. We should also remember that Jonathan Blanchard, the founder of Wheaton College, was one of the leaders against slavery. Charles Finney is usually thought of as a great evangelist. At Oberlin College, however, Finney did exactly the same thing as Blanchard did at Wheaton, calling for real change in the social order in regard to slavery. Both of them said without reservation that a law was wrong when it was wrong. Actually, both of these men called for civil disobedience if, and when, it was necessary. These men had a rich Christianity. It was a Christianity that understood the lordship of Christ, a lordship that extends across all of life. You simply cannot say Jesus is Savior without saying He is Lord. And He is not just Lord of the religious life. He is Lord over the totality of life as well.

Today, however, many evangelical Christians and evangelical leaders do not stress Christ's lordship in this way. For example, in *Whatever Happened to the Human Race?* in both the film and the book we stressed the lordship of Christ in regard to the legal issue concerning human life. Unhappily, at first this often was not accepted with enthusiasm. It is especially distressing that evangelicals and the evangelical leadership did not take a firm stand on abortion, because the unique dignity of human life is unbreakably linked to the existence of the infinite, personal God. There is a unique linkage between the concept of the dignity of human life and the existence of the infinite, personal God of the Judeo-Christian religion. Moreover, where this view has not been held, there has not been a high view of human life in general. As the West loses the concept of man being unique as made in the image of God, we are losing the concept of the dignity of human life as well. The abortion case, although important in itself, was only a symptom of a low view of human life that would have been unthinkable in the day when there was a Christian consensus in the United States. The high view of human life which we have taken for granted cannot be consistently held on the basis of final reality being material or energy, shaped by chance. As the materialistic, humanistic world view takes more and more control in such countries as the United States, we can be sure that the high view of human life will decrease and decrease. There is a natural progression from abortion, to infanticide, to the view put forth by some that the baby is not really human until a certain number of days after it is born, to euthanasia of the old. These things are not isolated issues. We as Christians should not be taken by surprise at all for they flow along as naturally as a flowing stream.

Thus, the issue is not abortion, important as that is, but

a low view of human life which is a natural result of the other total entity. Again, the lack of understanding of this is a clear example of not seeing the totals but looking only at the bits and pieces. The bits-and-pieces mentality has been with us so long that the church did not notice the shift from a Christian consensus to a humanistic consensus in our society. The church had taken the Christian heritage for granted for so long that Christians did not notice what was being lost.

What is ahead of us? I would suggest that we must have two tracks in mind simultaneously. First, with the conservative swing of the 1980 election, there is a window that is open. Let us pray that the window stays open, and not even just on an issue as important as human life, but that the total entity of the materialistic world view may be rolled back. We must take every opportunity to do this. We must not see, as in the past, only the bits and pieces. It will not be easy to roll back this humanistic entity because those holding that world view are deeply entrenched. They will use every measure at their disposal to see that the results they have achieved in all fields remain intact. But it is our task to change things at this very late hour.

But what if the window does not stay open? What if it closes? What then? If that happens, we must have a second track operating in our minds. In considering this other possibility, we must ask the question as to what percentage of people voted for a change in the last election out of principle and what percentage so voted because they thought it would increase their own personal peace and affluence. Nationally syndicated columnist George F. Will estimated that only twenty percent voted out of principle and "eighty percent for improved economic numbers no matter how provided."

If improved economic numbers are not forthcoming, what happens then? I do not believe there will be a swing to the old liberalism of the last fifty years. It has failed to produce the economic numbers. Instead, I believe that there will probably be some form of elite authoritarianism. All that would be needed in much of the West would be an illusion of what George Will called improved economic numbers. And as I wrote in *How Should We Then Live?* this would be especially so if it is brought in under the guise of constitutionality as it was done in the time of Caesar Augustus. If it is done this way, I do not think for most people there would be any concern. No one can be sure what form the elite would take. Various thinkers such as Daniel Bell and John Kenneth Galbraith have put forth a variety of concepts as to where and how the elite might arise. The basic concern, however, should not be the quarter from which the elite might arise. The mere possibility of such an elite should alarm us.

In the United States the courts, and especially the Supreme Court, with its avowedly sociological law, must be considered one possible candidate for an authoritarian elite. The courts acknowledge that they are now functioning on the basis of sociological law, and they not only rule on laws, but they make law. Moreover, the Supreme Court possesses the power to dominate the other two branches of government in the United States. This is awesome power.

Christians and the Christian institutions will feel increased power pushed against them if the dominance of the humanistic world view continues without resistance. Should we not be thinking and planning what to do about the present dominance of the humanistic world view and the even greater control which possibly lies ahead? The Christian theologians, the educators, the lawyers, and others have had a very poor average up to this point. We allowed the other total entity, the materialistic chance view of reality, to destroy what the founding fathers and the thirteen individual states had in mind when the country began. If we have run so poorly with the footmen, what will happen if we have to run with the horsemen?

It is time to think to the *bottom line* as our forefathers did. That is, what is the Christian's final relationship to the state? The modern materialistically oriented generation have no reason to obey the state except that the state has the guns and the patronage. This is not true of Christians. God tells us to obey the state. But does that mean that we are told to obey the state no matter what? Is that what the Bible says? Has God set up an authority in the state that is autonomous? In this area indeed is man the measure of all things? Not at all. The government as all of life stands under the law of God. When any office (e.g., husband, parent, church officer, employer, the state) rules what is contrary to God's law, it abrogates its authority. This was the position of the early church. The early Christians were killed because they refused to bow to Caesar. From the side of the Christians they died for religious reasons. From the view of the Roman State they died as civil rebels and political enemies because they were breaking the state law. It was an act of civil disobedience for which they went to their deaths.

We also must remember that at almost every point where the Reformation was successful there were elements of rebellion, political rebellion, involved. Samuel Rutherford formulated this concept in his *Lex Rex*. He would probably himself have been killed if he hadn't died first before the Scottish government could try him and have him killed. *Lex Rex* was banned in both Scotland and England because it said that God's law is King and that the king as well as the peasant was under the Scriptures. His book was seen as an act of rebellion.

John Locke secularized *Lex Rex*. His points were inalienable rights, government by consent, separation of powers, and the right of revolution—or stated another way, the right to resist unlawful authority. These were the points of Locke upon which Thomas Jefferson functioned.

John Witherspoon certainly knew Samuel Rutherford's writing well. The other founding fathers may or may not have known him, but they certainly knew Locke, and in both *Lex Rex* and Locke the view was presented that there comes a time where there must be disobedience on the *appropriate level*.

Of course, civil disobedience is a very serious and frightening matter. I want to emphasize two things. First, I am in no way talking about establishing a theocracy in name or in fact. That must be made completely clear. Second, there are so many emotionally and ideologically imbalanced people today that we must stress that civil disobedience must be exercised only on the appropriate level.

Samuel Rutherford spoke with care and in detail concerning the appropriate level of civil disobedience or resistance in *Lex Rex*. Rutherford, Locke, and the founding fathers had a *bottom line*. The thirteen colonies concluded that the time had come, and they disobeyed. Interestingly enough, the American colonists followed Samuel Rutherford's model and his safeguards concerning the appropriate level of resistance. The civil disobedience became a war and the United States of America was born. The basic question for them was not one of pragmatism, but one of principle. If there is no final place for civil disobedience then civil government is autonomous and has been put in the place of God. Our forefathers saw this clearly and resisted such tyranny.

It is time to think ahead in regard to the total problem, instead of always looking at only the bits and pieces. We must assert the biblical reality that when any office commands that which is contrary to God's law it abrogates its authority and, as such, it must be resisted on the appropriate level. We must not forget, however, that this is the second track. The first track is that we must take advantage of the window that is open at the present moment.

This means really taking advantage of it—not merely thinking and acting on bits and pieces but rolling back the false materialistic view of final reality. We must never forget that this view will naturally bring forth certain results which are not only relativistic and wrong, but also inhuman, as this view gives no basis for the uniqueness of Man.

Taking advantage of the possibilities before us means more than just taking political stands. It also means practicing all the possible Christian alternatives that are open to us. This is forcibly stressed in *Whatever Happened to the Human Race?* in regard to the problems of abortion, infanticide, and euthanasia. And we must practice Christian alternatives in all areas of human endeavor, even when it is costly.

If we put the necessary Christian alternatives into effect we cannot expect perfection. Man and the world are abnormal because of the fall. We can, however, bring substantial healing even now before Christ returns, looking to the risen Christ daily for our wisdom and strength. To say this does not mean that I am drawing back or lessening what I have said about our political responsibilities and our legal responsibilities. In the final analysis, however, it is not a question of political or legal responsibilities. It is a spiritual matter.

To fail to practice our legal and political responsibilities is less than living under the teaching of Scripture; and simultaneously, to fail to practice the Christian alternatives is equally less than living under the teaching of Scripture.

3 SECULARISM: TIDAL WAVE OF REPRESSION

William Bentley Ball

The term "frontier" suggests something distant—the farthest reach of a movement outward, like the Far West of yesterday or outer space today. But when we speak of religious liberty at this hour, we cannot characterize it as a push outward—a probing out beyond the citadel of the First Amendment in order to discover new ways to be free religiously. It is the other way around: the push, coming from the vast reaches of secularism, is inward. The citadel *is* the frontier, and the city which it guards is penetrated and in confusion.

It's all very well to describe the secularists (or secular humanists) as an invading force, as though to suggest fierce and disciplined regiments, but when we look at them we find not so much a regiment as a crowd. It is a tidal wave of a crowd, and it has its leaders, ranging from the forbidding types of totalitarianists found in Graham Greene and Orwell, the "barbarians in Brooks Brothers' suits" of whom John Courtney Murray spoke, to the little clerk in the leisure suit who only wants to help your church "get into compliance" with some preposterous new government regulation.

The tidal wave is produced by the spirit of the times—an age in which man is putting God out of his life and out of society. The result is that the great problems of mankind are now to be solved by secular means and for secular ends—the ends of material utility (as we see so well when we compare the attitudes of Christians and secularists with respect to euthanasia of Downs Syndrome children). With the secularist invasion has come a great confusion of tongues. The secularist will advocate "sterilization of the unfit," but the Christian asks, "unfit for what?" The prosecuting attorney in *Wisconsin v. Yoder* asked the Christian witness, Professor John Hostetler, "Isn't it the aim of education to help a child get ahead in the world?" And Professor Hostetler replied, "It all depends which world."

Today as we consider the constitutional frontier of religious liberty (the struggle taking place everywhere in our country) we must first understand why there can be no religious liberty in a secularist state, then recognize the prime theaters of action in the defense of religious liberty, and use the constitutional weaponry we have to defend religious liberty.

The Secularist State versus Religious Liberty

Secularism militates against religious liberty, and against personal freedoms generally, for two reasons. First, it does not recognize the existence of the "higher law"; second, that being so, secularism tends toward decisions based on the pragmatic public policy of the moment and tends to resist submitting those policies to the "higher" criteria of a constitution.

Our nation was organized under a "higher law" concept—the view that rights come from God. It is not accurate to say, as has Leo Pfeffer, that our Constitution is a secular document, because the true preamble to the Constitution is the Declaration of Independence, the birth-statement of our nationhood, and it says that rights come from God. If rights come from God, they do not come from the state or from society, or majorities, parties, consensuses, or the moment's "public policy."

Because the secularist view of man holds that rights come from society, i.e., the state, it therefore must hold that the state is superior in right to the individual, and will tend to be so irrespective of whether individuals' rights are spelled out in a constitution. Further, the necessities of the state being supreme, the power to achieve what is necessary is most conveniently placed in the hands of the administrators of the laws and stated in terms awarding them unlimited discretion, the guiding standards to them being such wide-open terms as "the public interest," "public necessity," "public policy." The achieving of those ends will be considered, in the language of contemporary constitutional law, a "compelling state interest" which overrides the assertion of any liberty protected under the Bill of Rights.

Notice two items of immeasurable breadth: the standard of "public policy" and the matching of discretionary power needed to effect "public policy." Compare now, two kinds of "compelling state interest"—the very familiar finite kind (as for example, when, in *Davis v. Beason,* the Supreme Court said that if your religion calls for human sacrifice, there is nevertheless a supreme state interest in barring that particular form of religious exercise) and the less familiar infinite kind (as, for example, when a court says that any form of a certain type of discrimination offends "public policy" and therefore must be barred in the name of a compelling state interest).

This mischief represents the reappearance in our day and in our land of the "reason of state" doctrine which took hold in Europe in the Seventeenth Century. Historically, the Christian jurisprudence of Europe (in spite of abuses) had recognized the principle of a rule of law to which was attached a special meaning. The king was subject to God, and the laws of the realm had to conform with immutable principles of justice and right derived from the Gospels. There was a "higher law" than the will of the ruler, and that higher law bound the ruler. This became corrupted in the Seventeenth Century by a new concept of rule of law, appearing initially in Botero's "Della Ragion di Stato"— "Concerning the Reason of the State." Its meaning was that the immutable principles may be breached by the state for reasons determined by the state. As Botero put it, "The reason of state is a necessary violation [*eccesio*] of the common law for the end of public utility." In this we see a shift from ethics to politics, whereas, in the Christian tradition of the law, Bracton and others had seen law as "an ordinance of reason" adopted for the common good. "Reason" for those thinkers embodied the will of God in human affairs. But the "reason of state" doctrine has right- ly been termed "a rational means for the accomplishing of metarational ends"—ends lying beyond those reasons which are based on theistic principle, and involving the irrational: the employment of force for the sake of the state, the destruction of God-given rights in the name of ends desired by the state. Two centuries later, the doctrine would be employed to perfection by the totalitarian states of the Twentieth Century.

Increasingly in our nation, the "reason of state" doctrine is crowding out the concept of constitutional liberty. In matters relating to religion, secularist promoters of the doctrine are nevertheless concerned—tactically, that is— lest they appear antireligious. They have two stock ploys in this connection. First, they (every government attorney I have ever faced in a religious liberty case) say that one is free to believe whatever one wishes; however, when one *acts* in the name of religion, the state's interests come first. I am always amused by this marvelous simplism: an

American is religiously free—inside his head! Be assured: the state does not want in. But *outside* his head, he'd better shape up, conform! Big Brother knows best. When we ridicule the secularist's presumption, he engages in a face-saver—his second ploy—which can be called the "religion under the steeple" ploy. Here the state lets one go a little beyond the confines of the head. One can have a church organization and a church edifice, can pray aloud, worship collectively. One can do things in the sacristy. One can do what the state calls (in the memorable phrase of the late U.S. Secretary of Labor, Mr. Marshall) "strictly religious." This is precisely the coercive position which Otto von Bismarck took in the *Kulturkampf* in 1872, and which France took in its Law of Separation of 1905. It is astonishing that this malevolent nonsense has been freely promoted in our own day not only by the U.S. Secretary of Labor, but also by the NLRB, the IRS, the Bureau of the Census, and innumerable state agencies.

Daily there are new evidences to substantiate the view that secularism, by its very nature, militates against religious liberty. Secularism may be a great institution, but some of us are not ready for an institution yet. Let's now turn to some cases presently in the courts wherein state secularism is being resisted.

The Main Theaters of Action
Four cases have impressed me as most threatening in terms of possible wide and extremely harmful impact. They are:

1. The *Bob Jones University* case, abuse of federal tax power;

2. The *Roloff* and *Shelton College* cases, licensing power;

3. *Dayton Christian Schools v. Ohio Civil Rights Commission,* sex discrimination rulings;

4. A composite of current court cases and some which are likely to be tested, denial of religious liberty in public institutions.

Abuse of the Federal Tax Power. The Fourth Circuit upheld IRS in its revocation of the tax exempt status of Bob Jones University on the ground that the University prohibits interracial dating and marriage to its students, both black and white. The court agreed that this prohibition was a part of the "religious teachings" of the institution, and the trial record leaves no doubt that that is so. We therefore begin consideration of the case with the established fact of a particular religious doctrine and practice. A second fact is clear in the trial record: that the University is pervasively religious. Third, the institution is shown to be absolutely private in the sense that it has been neither founded nor funded by government. The Fourth Circuit upheld the revocation of tax exemption on the ground that this was dictated by a compelling state interest in "eliminating all racial discrimination in education." The conclusion was based on two points: that the University is not simply "religious" but "religious" *and* "educational," and that the "public policy" of the United States does not countenance racial discrimination.

As to the first reason, the Fourth Circuit has apparently not caught up with the decisions of the Supreme Court in *Lemon v. Kurtzman* and *Meek v. Pittenger* which hold that schools indistinguishable in religious pervasiveness and regimen from Bob Jones University are not bifurcated institutions, part "religious" and part "secular" (which is what the Fourth Circuit meant when it said "religious *and* educational"). One wishes that the Fourth Circuit might have pondered those federal court decisions in the NLRB and unemployment compensation cases which, in accord with *Lemon* and *Meek,* have rejected the notion that private religious institutions may be commandeered for state uses by the trick of calling them (as did NLRB) "only partly religious" or (as did the late U.S. Secretary of Labor Marshall) "not strictly religious."

The "public policy" justification is even more loaded

with mischief. This the court derives from two wells—
both dry. The first is the famous opinion of Judge Leven-
thal in *Green v. Connally,* in 1971; the second comes from
the IRS. In *Green v. Connally* there were no religious
claimants and no Religion Clause claims were raised. That
is to say, no religious school has yet had its day in court. It
is beyond belief, therefore, that the Fourth Circuit would
go to *Green* as a source of its holding. It has really gone to
IRS as its most basic source. The court cites a long list of
IRS rulings and procedures, and then states:

> "The IRS later announced nationally that *it* would no longer
> allow charitable deductions . . . and tax exempt status . . . to
> racially discriminatory schools, including church-related
> schools."

The non-elected public servants of IRS have interpreted
Green to the nation and its courts and invented the conditions with which religious institutions must comply if they
are to keep the lifeline of tax exemption. We saw that
clearly in the Proposed Revenue Procedure attempted by
IRS two years ago and which is now carried into the May,
1980, order of the U.S. District Court for the District of
Columbia in the latest phase of *Green.* Here to perfection is
the "reason of state" doctrine, with its enforcing of stan-
dardless powers copiously assumed by an administrative
elite and made subject to their personal notions.

Many religious groups which do not agree with the
scriptural interpretation held by Bob Jones University
nevertheless see this case as important and threatening. For
example, the Catholic Hospital Association, in its national
newsletter, recently expressed concern over the case in
respect to the Catholic Church's requirement of an all-
male clergy.

Roloff, Shelton and Licensing. In both *State of Texas v.
Corpus Christi People's Baptist Church* (the so-called
"*Roloff*" case) and *New Jersey-Philadelphia Presbytery v.
New Jersey Board of Higher Education* the core issue is this:

Can government license a church? Put differently: Can a ministry exist without permission of the state? Put still differently: Can government impose a prior restraint upon religious witness? Texas and New Jersey have taken the position that (a) the state will determine what is and what is not a religious ministry, (b) if the allegedly religious activity has a "secular counterpart," then it may be subject to licensing. And licensing is *not* regulation. The states in question indeed desire to regulate, but they want even more: the power to say yes or no to the *existence* of a ministry.

We must pause over this matter of *power*. There exists the misapprehension among most regulators, and among too many attorneys, that if power is left unexercised, or is but benignly exercised, its mere existence is of no consequence. We need to hearken to what Chief Justice Marshall said in 1827: "Questions of power do not depend upon the degree to which it is exercised." And Madison who said in the Memorial and Remonstrance:

> . . . [I]t is proper to take alarm at the first experiment with our liberties. . . The free men of America did not wait till usurped *power* had strengthened itself by exercise, and entangled the question of precedent. They saw all the consequences in *the principle,* and they avoided the consequences by denying the principle. [emphasis added]

The churches in both the Texas and New Jersey cases have rightly resisted the very fact of a yes-or-no governmental power over their respective Christian ministries in child care and adult education. Much more is involved, however, in each of these cases. Each also presents the picture of *plenary governmental regulation*. And that body of regulation, found both in the statutes and in the regulations, is made plenary through the "reason of state" technique. In New Jersey, for example, all institutions of higher education must conform to a comprehensive range of so-called "standards" to guide state officials in determining whether a license shall issue. But in almost every

"standard" there is a word such as "adequate," "sufficient," or "satisfactory." The following excerpt reveals
who decides what these mean.

Adequate, appropriate, equivalent, significant, suitable,
and sufficient means adequate, appropriate, equivalent, significant, suitable, and sufficient, respectively, in the judgment
of the Chancellor or his representative and ultimately the
Board of Higher Education.

Here is *total* state control. Here is entanglement—indeed, envelopment. I am happy to report that the Third
Circuit, in an opinion filed April 14, characterized the
New Jersey regulations as suggesting "a very high degree
of state entanglement in Shelton [College's] religious
affairs."

The *Roloff* case contains the same constitutional problems—licensing, the state's definition of the Church's
ministry to distressed children as "secular," the myriad
regulations, and the accordion-like standards to be expanded or contracted at the personal will of state servants.
So comprehensive are those regulations that they encom-
pass the very dimensions of the morsels of food to be
consumed in a non-tax-supported, nongovernmentally
founded, private religious home for children. One standard, which the state's chief of licensing said was mandatory, provides that cheddar cheese is an allowable food,
but only "one thin slice" of cheddar cheese.

The New Jersey and Texas regulations also abound in
language which the states' chief administrators all found
(upon cross-examination) to be unintelligible. The Texas
standards, for example, contain this remarkable provision:
"If cheese is counted as milk, it should not be counted as
meat."

Here we are brought face to face with the enormously
important statement of the Supreme Court in the
Keyishian case:

The regulatory maze created . . . is wholly lacking in
"terms capable of objective measurement. . . ." [M]en of com-

mon intelligence must necessarily guess at its meaning and differ as to its application.

Or, as the Court said, an "in terrorem mechanism" especially to "those with a conscientious and scrupulous regard for such undertakings."

The Sex Discrimination Cases. Substantial case law is building up out of decisions under Title VII and other anti-discrimination provisions of law. Yet few areas are more fraught with significance to the Christian community than that of sexual differentiation. While Christians believe in justice to women and thus for equality in that sense, Christians do not agree with the teaching of ERA, that the sexes must be treated in the law as identical. Yet in cases such as *Dolter v. Wahlert High School,* 483 F. Supp. 266 (N.D. Iowa, E.D. 1980)—a memorably bad decision—it was held that a Catholic high school's code of religious moral conduct, as applied to a teacher who had violated that code by becoming pregnant as a result of premarital intercourse, violated Title VII and could "not be applied discriminatorily on account of sex"!

In the *Dayton Christian Schools* case, in which we now await a federal court decision, we find the state's effort to impose an Ohio statute making it an "unlawful discriminatory practice" for any employer

> . . . because of the . . . religion [or] sex . . . of any person to refuse to hire, or otherwise to discriminate against that person with respect to hire, tenure, terms, conditions, or privileges of employment, or any matter directly or indirectly related to employment.

This fantastic provision is a superb example of overbreadth. By its terms:

- St. John's Church (a Lutheran congregation) could not, solely on account of the applicant's religion, refuse to hire as pastor an individual of some other religious faith.

- Good Shepherd Convent (an Episcopal novitiate for nuns)

could not, solely on the ground that a teacher applicant was a Unitarian, refuse to hire that applicant.

● St. Mary's Seminary (a Roman Catholic seminary for training men for the priesthood) could not, solely on the ground of her sex, refuse to hire a woman as an instructor even though the Canon Law of the Catholic Church would forbid use of female instructors within the Seminary.

Much else unconstitutional resides in this sex discrimination statute—for example, the supposed exemptive provisions of bona fide occupational qualification. But that very provision imposes a prior restraint: a church has to go to the *state* "in advance" of the hiring of a staff member, for example, in order to determine whether that person's sex constitutes a bona fide occupational qualification. And that, in turn, involves all the issues of "public policy" and wide-openness of standards which we have seen in the other cases cited. There is a very wide range of practices or situations which can be clustered under the heading "sex discrimination"—various differentiations, some unfair, some protective, some dictated by a religious body's doctrinal teaching respecting man and woman. If all of these myriad and differing instances are to be swept up into the concept of compelling state interest by the device of saying that since they are all instances of "sex discrimination" and since "sex discrimination" offends "public policy," and that "public policy" is supreme, then constitutional liberty is paved over. The Constitution is a nullity. Again, this illustrates the mischief which resides in the idea of "public policy" as "compelling state interest." Many of the sex discrimination cases thus far have not been well defended, and the cement of bad case law precedent is starting to harden.

Religious Liberty in Public Institutions. Here, more than in any other area of our First Amendment law, bad precedent has been solidly established by the Supreme Court itself. The original source of the evil in the *McCollum* decision, and later reinforced by the rationale in *Engel* and *Schempp,* rests upon two false premises: that only the liberties of those who desire a religionless education may be accommodated, and that the resultant public school is not a secular humanist agency. All the myths and the factual vacuum upon which those decisions rested are seen, in the 1980s, in light of their consequences, both devastating and fortunate. The devastating consequences are seen in the rise of immorality and violence in our society along with, interestingly enough, a decline in intellectual competence. The fortunate consequence, so well described in the new Coleman Report, is seen in the reaction of the great proliferation of religious schools.

Yet the effects of *McCollum-Engel-Schempp* continue to militate against religious liberty in public institutions. We have seen many instances of denials of the slightest accommodation to religious freedom on public school and university campuses—denials of assembly to conduct religious services, to conduct religious study, to have chaplains. We see what are perhaps the effects of these decisions in the cultural and instructional programs within public elementary and secondary schools. The creationism conflict discloses a most obvious aspect of the narrowness of secular humanist dogmatism. And many programs in the public schools are secularist value-laden. For example, the aim of a public school program on "Sexuality and Family Life" is said to be "to produce a *mature person* capable of fulfilling his sexuality in the broadest sense . . . to develop *sound attitudes and values* to guide his sexual conduct . . . by imparting a *scientific* knowledge of all aspects of human sexuality." But who is a "mature person"? What is meant by fulfilling sexuality "in the broadest sense"? According to whose norm are the "attitudes and values" for the guiding of sexual conduct considered "sound"?

We need to confront denials of religious liberty in tax-supported institutions, but the confrontations must be the proper constitutional confrontations. Too often attorneys have advised clients to proceed on theories which either are inapposite or which actually confirm the negative principles as, for example, when a Bible program in a public school was defended on the grounds that the Bible is good literature and that reading the Bible promotes good citizenship. The attack for religious freedom in public institutions must not amount to a clever attempt to get God in under false pretenses. The attack must center specifically on religious liberty grounds and it undoubtedly will have to result in at least a partial overruling of *McCollum* and *Schempp*. The attack must be based upon a factual record of great breadth and depth. It will not neglect the areas of the Establishment Clause, rights of family privacy, and rights to know and learn.

Constitutional Responses for the Defense of Religious Liberty
We can envision defenses of religious liberty at the policy level, the jurisprudential level, and the level of litigation tactics. Under "policy" I would simply group what we, as Christians, need to be doing to change statutes, to get better statutes, to get good judges, to create affirmative media expression, to train leaders with Christian values, and in general to bring Christianity to bear on our culture. This Conference, and CLS, and the Center are splendid examples of what can be done as a leaven to our society.

My particular focus, however, is upon litigation as a means for the defense of religious liberty, and that involves what I have spoken of as the jurisprudential and tactical levels. Anyone who has litigated intensively in the area of the First Amendment must come to realize that our problems do not consist exclusively of particular interpretations of the Amendment. Our problem consists also of *more general* constitutional concepts, such as the unconstitutional delegation of legislative power and *ultra vires*. The first is where the legislature hands over its powers to agents through the conferral of regulatory power un-accompanied by strict standards. The second is where the agents make up powers on their own—assume powers not given them by the legislature. Under the first, the govern-ment of laws largely disappears and the government of men replaces it. Under the second, "homemade" law of the agents replaces the law of the people's elected repre-sentatives. We tend to think of these two sets of difficulties as matters once of some consequence in economic cases. What has begged for comment is the tremendous impact of these aberrations in terms of First Amendment liberties. Both unconstitutional delegation and *ultra vires* are appar-ent in the cases we have considered.

Why has this come about? We must find the answer, I believe, in the law journals and, more particularly, in the law teaching profession which (and I realize that this may be a gross generalization) have influenced legislatures and courts to put aside, as relics of the dead past, constitutional doctrine which once served to protect individual liberty, to foster representative government, and to restrain stat-ism. Compare the statement in 1871, in *Cooley's Constitu-tional Limitations,* with that of Professor Davis, in 1959, in his treatise on administrative law. Cooley said:

> One of the settled maxims in constitutional law is, that the power conferred upon the legislature to make laws cannot be delegated by that department to any other body or authority. Where the sovereign power of the State has located the au-thority, there it must remain; and by the constitutional agen-cy alone the laws must be made until the Constitution itself is changed. The power to whose judgment, wisdom, and pa-triotism this high prerogative has been intrusted cannot re-lieve itself of the responsibility by choosing other agencies upon which the power shall be devolved, nor can it substitute the judgment, wisdom, and patriotism of any other body for those to which alone the people have seen fit to confide this sovereign trust.

Professor Davis, on the other hand, states:

The notion that the courts must compel the legislative body to state an intelligible principle to guide all exercise of delegated power wrongly assumes that the only wisdom to be found in the various organs of government is entirely concentrated in the legislative body. Fundamentally, our system is not and never has been one of relying exclusively upon the legislative department for all development of policy. The executive and judicial branches of the government are and must be coordinate branches not only for carrying out policies determined by the legislative branch *but also for determining basic policy*.

The context of the Davis statement is economic cases. At least insofar as religious liberty cases are concerned, we will find much that is worth resorting to in the older parts of our American constitutional tradition. Fundamentally, in relation to personal liberty, the Constitution was aimed at restraint of the state. Today, in case after case relating to religious liberty, we encounter the bizarre presumption that it is the other way around; that the state is justified in whatever action, and that religion bears a great burden of proof to overcome that presumption. It is the job of Christian lawyers to destroy that presumption at every turn, to attack every vestige of the unwarranted assumption of power by government over religion, to be heard in the courts and in the legislatures—for those who cannot speak—in order to help reclaim our nation from secularism.

The voice must not be strident, but kindly and intelligent, and reflecting homework diligently done.

4 OPPOSING OUR IDOLATROUS CULTURE

Joel Nederhood

If we are to be useful to Jesus Christ, it is essential that we perceive the idolatrous nature of our culture and react as His followers by opposing it. If we understand the Bible's message, we will be able to recognize that the ancient forces of idolatry are as active today as they were when the Bible was written.

When we think about idols and about culture, we must do so on the most basic level and in the most fundamental terms. Clifford Geerts, an anthropologist, provides a useful definition of culture when he describes the essence of culture as a collection of shared meanings, common understandings regarding the particulars of social life and individual behavior. He asks, for example, "What does it mean in our culture . . . to work hard, to be successful, to own a Mercedes, to be a housewife, to be a real man, to fail, to be a homosexual, to have money, etc., etc?" The answers a society gives to such questions helps shape the cultural milieu in which its members live.

It is clear that culture is formed by forces that have

operated in the past and which combine with the cross-currents of the present to provide each of us with reference points for living which we use unconsciously to determine our own identity and that of others. These reference points also contribute to our convictions regarding duty and help us formulate standards for performance.

When we think about idolatry on a basic level, we must allow our ideas to be formed by the Bible. The Bible provides ample data regarding idolatrous culture, for its message and thrust can properly be viewed as directed against such culture. It may take some adjustment in our minds before we fully appreciate this characteristic of biblical material, for we are most accustomed to thinking about the Bible as God's revelation of Christ and salvation, which indeed it is; but in providing this revelation, it obliterates all ways of salvation which depend on false gods. The Bible is in fact a Spirit-inspired polemic designed with great precision to destroy the idolatrous culture which presently exists and that which existed at the time the Bible was written. The Bible is about idols and idolatrous culture through and through.

The Bible's preoccupation with the destruction of false religion, with idolatrous culture, becomes clear when one reviews the broad sweep of biblical data. Think of Moses and the Mosaic writings, for example. Isn't it striking that Moses was singularly equipped to cast the revelation of God in a form that devastated the idolatrous culture of his age?

Moses had learned about the religion of the covenant God of Israel from his mother's knee through a peculiar arrangement which required the acquiescence of his adoptive mother. And his knowledge of the true religion was perfected by his later friend-to-friend contact with the Lord. Moses also possessed firsthand knowledge of the prevalent religion of his age: as the son of Pharaoh's daughter he was instructed in the worldwide religion that originated in Mesopotamia and spread throughout the fertile crescent, the religion which was also expressed in Egypt's rituals.

We should not be surprised to find, therefore, a relationship between data in the Pentateuch and the religion of the East which dominated the world at the time Moses wrote; the relationship, however, is not one of similarity but of contrast. The idolatrous religion of that age is depicted as folly, and the religion of the God of Abraham and Isaac and Jacob is presented as the way of life in covenant. Just one example: in the religion of Babylon, the serpent was considered the source of wisdom, but in the biblical record, the true role of the serpent in mankind's misery is uncovered.

When one peruses the Old Testament with the battle between true religion and idolatry in mind, data abounds which fortifies the understanding that the Bible is about idolatry and it is against it through and through. The mention of Rahab in Psalms 87 and 89 has at least oblique reference to the god by that name in the Babylonian pantheon; surely this is the case in Isaiah 37 and 51. Indeed, Isaiah and Jeremiah engage in high ridicule of idolatry. Isaiah 44 is the classic picture of the woodcutter who uses part of the tree he has felled for burning and the other part for worshiping. In Jeremiah 10, the same figures of speech emerge, and idols are described as scarecrows in a melon patch (v. 5); the people of God are told: "Do not fear them; they can do no harm, nor can they do any good."

The New Testament depicts the triumph of the covenant religion of Israel over the idolatrous religion of the East. Isn't it breathtaking to find at the opening of Matthew's Gospel representatives of that very religion bowing in adoration before the infant Redeemer? In the life, death, and resurrection of Jesus the powers of darkness that had lent the false religion of idolatry its ersatz power were destroyed. Jesus' followers today now recognize that He has despoiled the principalities and powers of false religion, and following Him they unmask such religion for what it is and combat it with all of their gifts. For though the idols and the culture they defined were rendered ultimately powerless, there is a strength that remains to this present day.

We must not fail to notice that the New Testament depicts the man of God equipped for battle. And the Apostle John, who lived long enough to see the new idolatry which was opposed to Jesus develop, closed his first epistle with this admonition: "Dear children, keep yourselves from idols" (5:21).

The idolatry opposed by the Bible infused and defined culture—this is the reason why the true religion included so many specific prohibitions such as we find in the book of Leviticus; keeping oneself from idols involved not wearing clothes of the opposite sex and not cooking a kid in its mother's milk. Culture is always full of religion; it is the characteristic expression of a religious world view, and idols as such and specific liturgical events are only marks of a fuller, wider religious expression that can be discerned only when the total culture is analyzed. Today the idolatrous quality of our culture is expressed in the massive worship of the creature rather than the Creator, brought about by the ascendancy of the materialistic world view.

Evidence for the ascendancy of this world view is everywhere. The evolutionistic, naturalistic, materialistic world view is found in the presuppositions regarding human origins which undergird modern thought, it provides the framework for the education of most of our nation's children, it has infected the social sciences with its poison to the point where religion itself is explained in its terms. In jurisprudence this world view brought about the triumph of relativism as a sociological view of the law became dominant.

The prevalent world view states very simply that ultimate reality is material reality. This is purely and simply idolatry. What formerly was expressed crassly has now been transmuted into the teaching that goes on in the first grade, the university, and in law school. Christian men and women must see this clearly and seek to extricate themselves from it and oppose it; they must seek, as well, to create an alternative to this massive insult to Jesus. And it is not enough to retreat into the usual exercises of church and Sunday School: Christians must be active culturally *as Christians*.

How can they do this? How can we *do this?*

The first thing we must understand is that when it comes to religion the essential matter is fear. We will be able to act in a Christian way only if we are genuinely God-fearing rather than idol-fearing. The prophets help us see this when they call us not to fear what the nations fear (Isaiah 8:12) and not to be terrified by the signs in the sky that terrify the nations (Jeremiah 10:2). Instead, the people of God are to fear the Lord: "No one is like you, O Lord; you are great, and your name is mighty in power. Who should not revere you, O King of the nations? This is your due" (v. 6, 7). Surely, as we live this side of Pentecost the fear of the Lord should be a reality among all those who profess to be followers of Jesus.

If you want to know whether or not you are living in the service of the idolatrous culture that surrounds you or in the service of God, ask yourself this simple question: whom do I fear? Are you afraid of your colleagues? Of the government? Of your peers? Of your life-style? Remember, the nonbiblical world view has infiltrated every sector of culture, and Christians must earnestly examine themselves to make sure that they do not compromise their allegiance to Jesus in favor of some element in culture which they fear. It is very easy to entrust our security for eternity to God and our security for the present to the idols. If you seriously want to serve Jesus in connection with your profession, take up the question of fear on the deepest level and examine your conscience before the face of the Lord. And when you do that remember what Jesus said about this subject: "Do not be afraid of those who kill the body but cannot kill the soul. Rather, be afraid of the one who can destroy both soul and body in hell" (Matthew 10:28).

Lawyers who fear God rather than man have their work cut out for them. May I suggest three elements in our present idolatrous culture which need the attention of people who know that Jesus Christ is Lord? These are the three I am thinking about: the protection of human life, the structure of general education, and social justice.

First of all, we should recognize that the failure to protect life in the womb is an expression of a culture that has rejected God and chosen a naturalistic description of humanity. The view of human choice and the view of human sexuality which undergird the failure of our society to provide unborn children with the basic protections otherwise guaranteed by the Constitution are as firmly established as they are because of a failure to recognize how sacred a human being is. The revelation that man is the image bearer of God, which is basic to the Christian view of man, has been rejected by our culture, and a view of man as a part of the animal kingdom has displaced it. Those who fear God rather than the idols of this age have a pressing obligation to correct the hideous circumstances that now drench our nation in innocent blood. Though steadfast opposition to the current situation may illicit ridicule on the part of peers who expect attorneys to remain dispassionate, there is no question that such opposition is required by those who fear God. For the Bible forthrightly announces that God will not pardon those who persist in the shedding of innocent blood; He will most certainly follow such rebellion against His law with His judgment

(2 Kings 24:4). Clearly, this is a matter of fear—whom do you fear, God or man?

Secondly, we must address ourselves to the reforming of general education in our nation. And the reform must take place in the direction of pluralism; that is, we must break the monopoly now exercised by education that is formed by the evolutionary world view.

This is necessary because the idolatrous character of culture is nowhere more firmly entrenched than in education, and its future control of our society is guaranteed by its presence in the educational system. In the nature of the case, any culture reproduces itself in terms of its educational institutions, for they are the mechanisms which pass it on to the next generation. As conditions now stand, the only system of education which is judged worthy of support from the public treasury is a system which deliberately excludes the Christian world view and steadfastly promotes its opposite. God-fearing citizens cannot rest until a form of education which reflects the biblical perspective exists in our land without penalty and without prejudice, an alternative educational system which is available to all those who profess Christianity and who want their children educated in the fear of the Lord.

There should be no embarrassment in the pursuit of this goal caused by the charge that such an alternative form of education is religious while the established system is neutral with respect to religion. Those who are able to perceive the idolatrous nature of contemporary culture should have no difficulty perceiving, too, that the present educational establishment is thoroughly religious; the religion it represents is diametrically opposed to the religion of Christ. Therefore, those who fear God rather than the idols of this age must work with all diligence to achieve necessary educational reform.

And thirdly, those who fear God must work for social justice; by that I mean that they must earnestly seek conditions in our society which will insure that all citizens benefit equally from our common life together, and that all citizens exercise the responsibilities which are part of proper citizenship. Those who practice law cannot avoid this necessity by saying that their obligation is to their clients, and they are required simply to use the law to their clients' advantage. God-fearers must always have the broader picture in view, and the establishment of righteousness must be their primary objective.

I suppose that we would have to admit that by nature we are not interested in this exalted objective: our horizons are too close in, our little worlds too narrowly circumscribed. But the fear of the Lord and the disdain of idols can change us, for as we become more and more familiar with God's objectives we learn that our God is concerned about the plight of the poor and those who have been victimized by injustice. Once again it is the prophet Jeremiah who jolts us back to divine reality when he says: "Woe to him who builds his palace by unrighteousness, his upper rooms by injustice, making his countrymen work for nothing, not paying them for their labor" (22:13). A God-fearing attorney, obviously, will have to be committed to furthering the causes that are dear to the heart of God, and justice and righteousness are such causes.

I began by saying that if we are to be useful to Jesus Christ, it is essential that we perceive the idolatrous nature of our culture and oppose it. Our culture is most certainly in the grip of an enormous idolatry. Opposing all this in the name of Christ will take everything we are and everything we ever hope to be. But of course that's the way it is with being a Christian.

"For great is the Lord and most worthy of praise; he is to be feared above all gods. For all the gods of the nations are idols, but the Lord made the heavens" (Psalm 96:4, 5).

5 THE ORIGINS OF LIBERTY IN LAW

Robert L. Toms

When the great lawgiver Moses brought the Ten Commandments down from the mountain, mankind received a codified constitution. It is probably no accident that the first commandment is "Thou shalt have no other gods before Me." Perhaps the most dangerous philosophical idea in our time, and of all time, is that there is no "right" and therefore no wrong—that rights are our own creation, and are not a part of the objective order.

Not only is this idea dehumanizing, but its acceptance leads to the conclusion that there is no limitation on the power of a sovereign, since it would follow that might makes right, not right makes right. The Nazi holocaust and the casting adrift of people to starve in Asian waters are but two examples of unlimited power.

This idea that absolute truth does not exist has penetrated our society and our law. The great Justice Oliver Wendell Holmes wrote that "truth is the majority vote of that nation that could lick all others." He said further, ". . . so when it comes to the development of a *corpus juris,* the ultimate question is what do the dominant forces of a community want, and do they want it hard enough to disregard whatever inhibitions stand in the way."

In contrast, the French Christian lawyer-philosopher Jacques Ellul, tempered by years of teaching law, by practical experience as an elected politician, and by working underground against the Nazis, warns us, "Day after day the wind blows away the pages of our calendars, our newspapers, and our political regime, and we glide along the stream of time without a judgment, carried about by 'all winds of doctrine' on the current of history, which is always slipping into the perpetual past. Now we ought to react vigorously against this slackness, this tendency to drift. If we are to live in this world, we need to know it far more profoundly, we need to rediscover the meanings of events and the spiritual framework which our contemporaries have lost."

Human rights are the subject of the tongue and pen of every law scholar, politician, and thinking citizen in our contemporary society. Human rights are being given more attention now than at any time in history. Ancient civilizations rarely recognized or articulated human rights, even in a fragmentary sense. Most recorded societies did not clearly recognize that a human being has a unique personality endowed with self-consciousness and a free will. In the stream of Judeo-Christian history and philosophy, and after the coming of Christ and God's revelation through the Scriptures, the idea became clear that each man and woman, by the fact of his or her humanity, whether high-born or low-born, slave or free, man or woman, old or young, educated or uneducated, privileged or unprivileged, black, white, yellow or brown, had an individual bargain to make between the Creator and himself, and the fate of his or her life and soul is dependent upon an individual act of conscience and choice. This radical concept made each person completely responsible for his or her actions, established a freedom of choice, and created conceptually direct privity between each person and God. Of significance here is the concept that the state, the monarch, the dictator, the tribal leader, was no longer a deity to be obeyed unquestionably or for whom one should die or forfeit goods or family. Rather, the ruler became a temporary delegatee of temporal power under the jurisdiction of the Maker of heaven and earth. In centuries of despotism in both the West and the East, where the mass, the group, the tribe or the state had been the ultimate authority, where man had no identity except what he could contribute to the whole, this was an extremely radical philosophical view. In the dark and middle ages the preservation of religious faith by the church gave men and women moral individuality, but society still stripped them of it wherever it had the power to do so.

Gradually, as modern law systems took shape, the concept of the Rule of Law emerged, a rule which could be invoked against even the ruler on behalf of an individual. And so in the early records of our common law, we see the emerging of such petitions and concepts as the Petition of Right in 1628 from which the framers of our Constitution took "due process of law," the Agreement of the People in 1649, providing for a representative Parliament, and the Habeas Corpus Act of 1679. Out of these petitions came our Habeas Corpus, the Standing Army Clause, the Quartering of Soldiers Clause, and others. This spirit of freedom matured through the history of the English-speaking people, and emerged in a new and clearer form in our Declaration of Independence. The violence in English history prior to this period of history spurred the founders of our republic to draft limitations in the Constitution on both the executive department and the legislative department, an experience unique in the history of men and government. At that time, Jefferson wrote, "In question of power, then, let no more be heard of confidence in man, but bind him down from mischief by the chains of the Constitution."

What is liberty? Liberty is given exceptional importance in the Preamble to the Declaration of Independence. In fact, it says that rather than liberty be destroyed, the government itself shall be swept away and the people shall "institute new government, laying its foundation on such principles and organizing its power in such form as to them shall seem most likely to affect their safety and happiness."

Liberty, according to John Stuart Mill, is "the aim of patriots to set limits on the power which the ruler should be suffered to exercise over the community." Liberty, then, is a limitation on power, and where the limitation is proper, there is liberty, and where it is not, liberty is lost. This concept underlies all the great documents of freedom. For example:

In the Magna Carta in 1215 King John "granted to all the free men of our kingdom for us and our heirs forever all the underwritten liberties, to be had and holden by them and their heirs of us and our heirs forever."

The Habeas Corpus Act of 1679 was "for the better securing of the liberty of the subjects."

The Instrument of Government of 1653 for England, Scotland and Ireland spoke regarding "all laws, statutes and ordinances and any clauses in any law, statute or ordinance to the contrary of the aforesaid liberty shall be esteemed as null and void."

The American Declaration of Rights of 1774 said in part, ". . . in order to obtain such establishment as that their religion, laws and liberties may not be subverted." The first resolution was that they "are entitled to life, liberty and property," and "that they have never ceded to any sovereign power whatever a right to dispose of either without their consent."

In the Declaration of Independence liberty was declared

to be "inalienable," that is, one could not even consent to part with it and lose it for himself or his children and posterity.

In the Virginia Bill of Rights it was said "that all men are by nature equally free and independent and have certain inherent rights of which when they enter into a state of society, they cannot by any compact deprive or divest their posterity, namely, the enjoyment of life and liberty with the means of acquiring and possessing property and pursuing and obtaining happiness and safety."

Many of our framers had studied Blackstone's *Commentaries,* and in his lectures at Oxford he had said, "This natural liberty consists properly in a power of acting as one thinks fit without any restraint or control, unless by the Law of Nature, being a right inherent in us by birth and one of the gifts of God to man at his creation when He endowed him with the faculty of free will."

All of our individual freedoms are tied inextricably to freedom of religion. The freedom to relate to God or to no God is a matter of individual conscience, as is engaging in duties arising from that relationship or abstaining from practices according to one's conscience. If government interferes in that process, it is the beginning of the end of liberty.

Recently, I watched on television the Columbia space shuttle land in the California desert. As that space vehicle had soared into the heavens my thoughts soared as I contemplated the great wonders of our scientific exploration of the universe. I'm a science enthusiast and I enjoy reading even fictionalized versions. One of the most exciting books I have read is *The Dragons of Eden,* which won the Pulitzer Prize. In it Carl Sagan explores the incredible wonders of the human mind and human creativity. However, at the end of the book, when he gets to religion, he reflects an established and all-too-popular view in our society: "There is today in the West a resurgence of interest in vague, anecdotal and often demonstrably erroneous doctrines which imply an intellectual careless-ness, and absence of tough-mindedness, and a diversion of energies not very promising for our survival." Then he lists these doctrines which he calls "dream protocols" and he includes "astrology, the Bermuda Triangle mystery, flying saucer accounts, ancient astronauts, pyramidology, the emotional lives and musical preferences of geraniums, . . . and the doctrine of specific creation by God or gods of mankind."

Let me ask, if Sagan is right, whither goes the "en-dowed by his Creator with inalienable rights"? From where, from whom, and how defendable are the human rights we talk about? And, if human rights are derived from the ideas of men, who can judge with authority the laws they may enact from what they believe is their irre-sistible scientific basis?

Unfortunately, the modern scientific and pseudo-scientific doctrines are supported by what C. S. Lewis called "the irresistible scientific technique of the man-molders of the new age." While these views are popularly accepted, the exclusion of faith has neither a logical nor experimental foundation. It is a philosophical and not a scientific judgment. Now even science no longer excludes faith. Recognizing the importance of intuition, science has moved with great progressive leaps in quantum physics, relativity, and other correctives to our previous knowl-edge. From error to knowledge to error to knowledge, scientists have increasingly seen that they also cannot be morally neutral. They face such questions as, How and by what standards do we control atomic fusion and genetic engineering? How do we build values into the use of sci-ence?

The Swiss physician Paul Tournier sums it up. "The present age appears to be in the final crisis of modern times, characterized by dichotomies between the spiritual and the temporal. Tired of partial solutions, tired of material progress which does not deliver it from spiritual anguish, tired of intellectual dialectics which become incarnated in real life, humanity yearns for the recovery of the unitary concept of man in the world. Since it is not willing to return to the Christianity from which it has been estranged for several centuries, it plunges desperately into all kinds of contradictory ideologies which claim to be able to solve the problems. After trying so many false solutions, will it finally be able again to face the true one? Will the Christian churches be capable of responding to this confused yearning of the modern world? It will be certainly necessary to find a new harmony between the church and society, between the spirit and the body. . . . This rift between the spiritual and the temporal not only divides the world in general, but also disturbs the inner harmony of every one of us. We need to close that gap between ourselves before we can help the world to do so. It is not only a matter of concept and ideas and questions of the intellectual in the narrower sense, but rather of the Lordship of Jesus Christ over our whole life. The church must proclaim, but it also must show, when a businessman really wants to be honest, when the physician really respects a human person, when an artist seeks his inspiration in God, when a lawyer applies his faith in his profession."

We need to rediscover the spiritual roots of our lives and our law, to examine the areas of stress in law and society, to discover strategies to strengthen the social fabric for the free practice and belief of religion in our time. We must ask, as Lincoln did at Gettysburg, Will freedom endure in the exigencies of this age?

We must obtain knowledge of ourselves, our society, and our law. We must settle our relationship with our God and clearly articulate our faith. We must respect the person and rights of those who differ with us, and whose search for God we believe has led them astray. We must build a sound arsenal of jurisprudence to preserve sure foundations of liberty. We must guard all frontiers of liberty from enslavers in any guise. But, most of all, we must do all of this as redemptive servants of Christ, stilling the chaotic, stormy waters of contemporary life and law, and be agents for the discovery of a jurisprudence of hope. A unifying hope is what the world needs and our law needs, and we can provide it by appropriating the grace, peace, and power of the Gospel.

6 RELIGIOUS FREEDOM: THE DEVELOPING PATTERN OF RESTRICTION

Dean M. Kelley

Government Intervention in Religious Affairs was the title of a significant conference in Washington, D.C. It was sponsored by six major national religious bodies representing ninety percent of the adherents of organized religion in the United States. They were The National Council of Churches, The United States Catholic Conference, The Synagogue Council of America, The Lutheran Council, The National Association of Evangelicals and The Southern Baptist Convention.

With the participation of a number of other national bodies unaffiliated with these six, but invited by them—the Mormons, the Christian Scientists, the Seventh-day Adventists, the Salvation Army, the Unitarians, the Scientologists, the Sikhs, the Unification Church, and the Hare Krishnas—the conference represented the most inclusive gathering of religious people in the history of the country.

Why did they come together? Because they were concerned about a common problem: the developing pattern of government intervention in religious affairs. The chairman outlined seventeen evidences that suggest there is a growing tendency on the part of government authorities at state and federal levels to regulate religious bodies that were formerly immune from such attentions. The seventeen instances cited are:

1. Efforts by state and local governments to regulate fund-raising by religious bodies
2. Efforts to require religious bodies to register with and report to government officials if they engage in efforts to influence legislation (so-called "lobbying disclosure" laws)
3. Efforts by the National Labor Relations Board to supervise elections for labor representation by lay teachers in Roman Catholic parochial schools (which have been halted by the U.S. Supreme Court)
4. Internal Revenue Service's definition of "integrated auxiliaries" of churches that tends to separate church-related colleges and hospitals from the churches that sponsor them and to link them instead to their "secular counterparts"
5. Attempts by state departments of education to regulate the curriculum content and teachers' qualifications in Christian schools (which have been halted by state courts in Ohio, Vermont, and Kentucky, but upheld in Nebraska, Wisconsin, and Maine)
6. Attempts by federal and state departments of labor to collect unemployment compensation taxes from church-related agencies that hitherto were exempt, as churches are
7. Imposing by the (then) Department of Health, Education and Welfare of requirements of coeducational sports, hygiene instruction, dormitory and off-campus residence policies on church-related colleges (such as Brigham Young University) which have religious objections to mingling of the sexes in such ways
8. Efforts by several federal agencies (Civil Rights Commission, Equal Employment Opportunities Commission, Department of Health and Human Services, Department of Education) to require church-related agencies and institutions, including theological seminaries, to report their employment and admissions statistics by race, sex,

and religion, even though they receive no government funds, with threats to cut off grants or loans to students unless they hire faculty, for instance, from other religious adherences

9. Sampling surveys by the Bureau of the Census of churches and church agencies, requiring them to submit voluminous reports under penalty of law, even though the Bureau admitted to a church attorney that it had no authority to do so, but refused to advise churches that they were not required to comply

10. Grand jury interrogation of church workers about internal affairs of churches

11. Use by intelligence agencies of clergy and missionaries as informants

12. Subpoenas of ecclesiastical records by plaintiffs and defendants in civil and criminal suits

13. Placing a church in receivership because of allegations of mismanagement of church funds made by dissident members

14. Granting by courts of conservatorship orders allowing parents to obtain physical custody of (adult) offspring out of unpopular religious movements for purposes of forcing them to abandon their adherence thereto

15. Withdrawal by IRS of tax exemption from various religious groups for failure to comply with "public policy"

16. Determination by IRS of what is "religious ministry" by clergy to qualify for exclusion of cash housing allowance from taxable income (often in contradiction to the religious body's own definition of "ministry")

17. Redefinition by the civil courts of ecclesiastical polity, so that hierarchical bodies are often in effect rendered congregational with respect to their ability to control local church property, and dispersed "connectional" bodies are deemed to be hierarchical with respect to their ostensible liability for torts committed by local entities, contrary to their own self-definition in both cases

The seriousness of these incursions is reflected by the fact that in at least *five* such areas some of the most staid and conservative religious bodies have formally and officially adopted a policy of *deliberate civil disobedience*.

Brigham Young University, operated by the Church of

Jesus Christ of Latter-day Saints (Mormon), refused to comply with HEW regulations requiring non-discrimination by sex in off-campus residence accommodations for students; HEW backed down.

Several bishops of the Roman Catholic Church refused to comply with a National Labor Relations Board order that they permit unionization of lay teachers in parochial schools. The NLRB took them to court, and two circuit courts of appeals held that if such schools are too religious to receive public funds, they are too religious for a federal agency to regulate. The U.S. Supreme Court did not go that far, but simply held that Congress had not given the NLRB authority to intervene in church-related schools (*NLRB* v. *Catholic Bishop of Chicago,* 440 U.S. 490, 1979).

Southwestern Baptist Theological Seminary, operated by the Southern Baptist Convention, has refused to comply with requirements of the Equal Employment Opportunities Commission that it file form EEO-6 reporting its employment data. The seminary prevailed in the federal district court, which ruled that EEOC does not have jurisdiction over it. The Circuit Court reversed, and the case is being taken to the Supreme Court (*Equal Employment Opportunities Commission* v. *Southwestern Baptist Theological Seminary*). (This case was reported to the conference in detail by James E. Wood, Jr., Editor of the *Journal of Church and State,* Baylor University, Waco, Texas.)

Concordia College and other schools of the Lutheran Church–Missouri Synod are refusing to file annual informational returns (Form 990) required by Section 6033 of the Internal Revenue Code, which provides a mandatory exemption for "churches, their integrated auxiliaries, and conventions and associations of churches." The Synod contends that its colleges are integral to its mission and thus exempt from filing. This case will soon be in the courts. It was reported to the conference by Philip E. Draheim, of St. Louis, Mo., attorney for the Synod.

An even more conservative body, the Wisconsin Evangelical Lutheran Synod, has challenged the decision by the U.S. Secretary of Labor that "church-related" schools would no longer be exempt from payment of unemployment tax on their employees, even if they are hired, directed and paid by the church itself. Nine courts have rejected the Secretary's interpretation, but a tenth, the South Dakota Supreme Court, upheld it, and the U.S. Supreme Court reversed, at least as to schools not separately incorporated (*St. Martin's Evangelical Lutheran Church* v. *State of South Dakota*).

In addition, innumerable evangelical churches which operate Christian schools or child-care institutions have been resisting state regulation with varying degrees of success. The keynote speaker at the conference, William Bentley Ball, an attorney from Harrisburg, Pa., has represented many of them, usually successfully. He spoke on "Government as Big Brother to the Churches" pointing to the penchant of legislators to write overbroad and ill-defined laws, and of administrators to amplify them with even more expansive regulations, and then benignly to assure church agencies that they don't have to comply with *all* of the requirements (no one could), but to make a "good faith" effort at "substantial" compliance. How much is that? No one can say—in advance. But the administrator retains the discretion to determine—*after* the fact—that compliance has not been adequate.

The purpose of law is to enable everyone affected to determine in advance how to *obey* it. That is especially important, the Supreme Court has said (*Keyishian* v. *Board of Regents,* 384 U.S. 589, at 604, 1967) in areas afforded the protection of the First Amendment. Yet that is the area where churches are increasingly subject to the undelineated whim or caprice of government administrators.

In addition to Mr. Ball, Dr. Wood, and Mr. Draheim, other outstanding scholars and practitioners in the field of church-state law offered observations and insights.

Lawrence Tribe of the Harvard Law School, a distinguished authority on *American Constitutional Law* (that's the name of his major work, a standard reference in courts and law schools), noted that religious bodies are one of several kinds of entities that enjoy a special, privileged status under the Constitution. Others include Indian tribes, the press, political parties and the family. He recommended, however, that religious bodies, wherever possible, not rely on that special status but appeal to broader rights, such as freedom of speech, press, and association in order not to trigger resentments.

Father Charles Whelan, S.J., Professor of Constitutional Law at Fordham University Law School and Associate Editor of *America* Magazine, spoke on the use (or misuse) of trust theory in church property disputes and in the recent efforts by the Attorney General of California to supervise the activities of churches under the contention that they are "public trusts." Father Whelan did not dispute their being charitable trusts or charitable corporations, but concluded that their being *churches* does not make them *more* accessible to supervision than business corporations but far *less*.

Sharon Worthing, an attorney in private practice in New York and a member of the advisory board of Americans United, gave *two* papers, one pointing out the potential for government surveillance of religious organizations under statutes which require data to be reported to various state and federal agencies. If the data was consolidated in one computer, the government(s) would know a great deal about the internal affairs of churches. The other paper reported on the use of conservatorship proceedings as a state-sanctioned technique for legitimizing the forcible deconversion (or "deprogramming") of members of unpopular religious groups (often stigmatized as "cults").

Wilfred Caron, General Counsel of the United States Catholic Conference, with two of his colleagues, reported on growing instances of governmental restraint on political activities of religious bodies, as in IRS restrictions on the publication of incumbent legislators' voting records by Section 501 (c) (3) organizations, including churches. (His organization had itself recently been made a party defendant in a suit by Abortion Rights Mobilization to compel the Commissioner of Internal Revenue to revoke the tax exemption of the Catholic Church because of alleged lobbying and electioneering to prevent public funding of abortion under Medicaid.)

Eugene Scheiman, an attorney in private practice in New York City, reported on the court use of compulsory process to obtain information about the internal affairs of churches, as in grand jury proceedings, discovery orders and subpoenas. He contended that the priest-penitent privilege is the core rather than the circumference of a broader privilege which should protect church workers (not just clergy) from being compelled to disclose information gained through their work in the church, lest such disclosure dissolve the relationships of confidence and trust without which the churches' work is paralyzed by fear of informers.

Barry Fisher, an attorney in private practice in Los Angeles, reported on the increasing efforts by attorneys general to clamp down on charitable solicitations, including those of churches, by requiring them to register with a government official and report to him/her all of their financial data. He cited a number of such statutes that had been struck down on behalf of some of the new religious movements (who were also represented at the conference by two or three registrants each).

Stanley Weithorn, author of the (now seven-volume) *Tax Techniques for Foundations and Exempt Organizations,* spoke on "Frontier Issues of Tax Exemption for Religious Organizations." Two areas were of particular interest to him: the use of the "private inurement" test to exclude from the exempt category certain collectivist religious communities which provide food, clothing and shelter for all their members as an incidental aspect of their shared religious life, and the application of the "public policy" test to exempt organizations, most recently in the *Bob Jones University* case, a test for which there is no statutory basis. (The chairman of the conference suggested at the end that various religious bodies, even if they disagreed vehemently with Bob Jones University's rule against interracial dating by students, which IRS maintained violated "public policy" and disqualified the University for tax exemption, might nevertheless want to file *amicus* briefs in opposition to the government's effort to use tax exemption as a stick to punish exempt organizations who were thought to be acting contrary to the "public policy" of the day.)

As a corrective to what some thought might be too much of a "Lemme Alone" thrust of the conference, William Lee Miller, professor of political science and of religious studies at Indiana University, gave a paper entitled, "Responsible, Democratic Government, Not Religion, Is the Endangered Species," in which he urged churches not to join the chorus of special interests crying, "Get the government off our backs!"

The conference concluded with a paper by Marvin Braiterman, Professor of Law and Public Policy at New England College, and Dean M. Kelley, Director for Religious and Civil Liberty of the National Council of Churches, entitled, "When Is Governmental Intervention *Legitimate*?" They pointed to a "parade of horribles": clear instances of crimes perpetrated by "religious leaders" which no one would want to go unpunished. Belonging to a religious organization does not—or should not—shield anyone from punishment who commits a crime, but the same threshold of evidence must be met before a person or group can be investigated—whether religious or not. Religious groups should not think of themselves as "above the law." They are *under the law,* and so is the government. Both are bound by the basic law of the nation which created a special category *under the law* for religion, which both government and religion are duty-bound to respect. The role of government with respect to religion, the paper contended, should be *minimal.* It should be limited to those instances which can be justified by a "compelling state interest" that can be served in no other way, such as protection of "public health and safety," and it urged the hearers to press the courts to make that test increasingly stringent, a direction the Supreme Court seems to be moving in this decade.

The chairperson expressed in his opening and closing statements that the incursions by government into the realm of religious activities were not the result of a conspiracy by government to "get" the churches, but was simply the ineluctable and mindless propensity of the bureaucrat (which is not limited to government) to systematize, regularize and extend its jurisdiction over broader and broader areas without regard to limitations imposed by the Constitution. They often act, not at their own motion, but at the behest of people who are uneasy about the activities of religious groups.

The remedy is not to view the government as the "enemy" or to mount an all-out war against it, but to say, in a firm but friendly way, "Thus far, and no farther." In most cases the government has acceded (eventually) to that stand. Occasionally a pitched battle must be fought, and there all religious organizations have a common interest, lest some particularly vulnerable group give way and lose terrain that is important to all.

It is a truism of civil liberties law that everyone's rights and freedom are often at stake in cases involving groups we would rather not defend, since government rarely takes on the large and well-respected churches until it has obtained advantageous precedents over marginal or unpopular groups. So we often need to uphold religious liberty on behalf of new religious movements that are not yet widely understood or accepted.

An example of such a situation is the plethora of so-called "anti-cult" or "anti-Moonie" bills now pending in eight or nine state legislatures. Some may think that they provide a useful curb on unscrupulous and opportunistic recruiting tactics, but they really are anti-*conversion* bills that would apply equally to converts of more conventional religious bodies. The New York version begins:

> A court of competent jurisdiction shall have power to appoint one or more temporary guardians for any person sixteen years of age or older, upon a showing that:
> (a) The person has undergone a sudden and dramatic personality change which is identifiable by the following characteristics:
> 1. Abrupt and drastic alteration of basic values and lifestyle, as contrasted with gradual change such as that which might result from maturation or education;

The bill is obviously written and backed by people who are upset by the prospect of conversion, who view it as abnormal and explicable only by outside manipulation or "mind-control" and want a legal means to *undo* it. In some circles an illegal method of forcible abduction called "de-programming" has been used which consists of round-the-clock browbeating and harassment until the victim abandons his/her newfound religious convictions. This bill is designed to legitimate that violation of religious liberty! The bill continues:

> 2. Lack of appropriate emotional response. [How would people who want to take away your religion define *appropriate* emotional response?]
> 3. Regression to childlike behavior.

The bill goes on to list physical changes such as in weight, hair or expression, a reduction of decisional capacity, such as judgment, or psychopathological changes such as dissociation or hallucinations. There follows a list of techniques which, according to the bill, result in personality changes. These include: isolation from family and friends, control over information, physical debilitation through such means as depriving of sleep and adequate diet, and mental debilitation by inducing anxiety, guilt, fear and dependency. (The bill generously adds that the petitioner need not "show the existence of each and every characteristic" described.) Much of the description could apply not only to conversion to any religion, but to entry into a convent or monastery, or following an especially intensive summer experience at church camp, or to the regimen at Weight Watchers, Alcoholics Anonymous, boot-camp or medical school. Yet such characteristics are to be the basis for the court's authorization of a "temporary guardianship" during which the victim is to be subjected to a plan of treatment "under the supervision of a licensed psychiatrist, psychologist or psychiatric social worker" and not "solely for the purpose of altering the political, religious or other beliefs of the person," but "to enable the person to make informed and independent judgments."

Not only does the bill provide that the petitioner may go *judge-shopping* until a cooperative judge is found, but neither the petitioner nor the prospective victim need have any previous connection with New York State except to appear in one of its courts. It would have the effect of giving the temporary guardian *physical custody* of the *person* of the victim, unlike existing laws governing civil commitment, which is made to an *institution*. Moreover, the U.S. Supreme Court has said that such commitment is unconstitutional unless the person is an *actual danger to himself or others*, of which no showing is required in this bill! (*O'Connor* v. *Donaldson*, 422 U.S. 563, 1975).

This digression is to illustrate in a concrete way that there are "developing patterns of restrictions on the collective free exercise of religion." There are apparently people who see religion—of any intense or effective kind—as a peril that must be tightly controlled.

The tragedy at Jonestown has added fuel to that fire and is cited every time someone wants to impose restrictions on religion. Or the specter of the "cults" is trotted out, and they are charged with all the misdoings that have been alleged against new religious movements in every age, including the Black Muslims, the Jehovah's Witnesses, the Mormons, the followers of John Wesley, clear back to the early church founded by Jesus Christ. Each time the conventional, accepted, familiar religious groups are assured, "This doesn't apply to *you*," but we should not be lulled into a false sense of security by that assurance, because it *does* spread to *all* religious groups if left unchecked. Even the most dedicated civil libertarians seem to be susceptible to the temptation of viewing any but the most docile and inobtrusive kind of religion with suspicion. Your classic John Stuart Mill-type civil libertarian can defend freedoms exercised by individuals in dispersion pretty well, but when those freedoms are *religious,* he tends to get very *nervous.* And when they are exercised *collectively* by those sharing the same religious faith, he begins to *climb the wall!*

That is why it is so important that organizations like Christian Legal Society exist, to understand and appreciate what real religion is and does, and the need for its collective free exercise, not only for the fulfillment of religious adherents but for the survival of society itself, which is in jeopardy if most people do not have a way of "making sense" of their lives most of the time. Religion is what does that, and so society as a whole has an important (secular) stake in the maximum protection for the collective free exercise of religion.

7 USING THE CONSTITUTION TO DEFEND RELIGIOUS RIGHTS

Bernard Zylstra

In order to address the question of the impact of law on religious expression and freedom, it is appropriate to begin with the meaning of *law*. Webster defines it as "the whole body of . . . customs, practices, or rules constituting the organic rule prescribing the nature and conditions of existence of a state or other organized community." This "organic rule" allocates the rights, duties, freedoms and privileges in the state or other organized community. The key word here is *right*, for we are concerned with the rightful expression of religion in society.

The civilization of the West is the heir of the Roman law definition of right, viz. *suum cuique tribuere*, to render to each his due. But what is one's due? To what does one have a right? What is a just claim which, by way of the public legal system, one can expect society to meet? Questions like these are asked each day by politicians and parliamentarians, by theorists and theologians, but particularly by the poor, the prisoners, the persecuted. Answers are not nearly as numerous as the questions. Nonetheless, answers are constantly given in the way societies distribute resources and in the philosophies of the world's great thinkers. Aristotle argued that persons have a natural right to an equal share of society's wealth—though he immediately made distinctions between proportionate and numerical equality.[1] John Locke asserted that one has a right to what he has worked for. And Karl Marx stated that one has a right to what he needs.

All of these conceptions of justice contain an element of truth. We intuitively sense that equality, merit and need are basic components of justice. But the singling out of one component as the key factor in justice illustrates the dependence of these conceptions on different world views. How, then, should the Christian deal with conceptions of justice in the context of non-Christian patterns of life and thought? I believe that the partial insights of both pagan and secular thinkers can be meaningful in the development of a view of justice built on the biblical world view. The Bible pictures the world as God's good creation, fallen into sin, and now in the cosmic process of redemptive restoration because of Christ's substitutionary death and the Spirit's regenerative work in the hearts of men and women. A biblical conception of justice reflects this threefold picture of creation, fall, and redemption.[2] It begins by taking seriously the biblical teachings on creation. Here Emil Brunner is helpful.

> The Christian conception of justice . . . is determined by the conception of God's order of creation. What corresponds to the Creator's ordinance is just—to that ordinance which bestows on every creature, with its being, the law of its being and its relationships to other creatures. The "primal order" to which every one refers in using the words "just" or "unjust," the "due" which is rendered to each man, is the order of creation, which is the will of the Creator made manifest.[3]

H. G. Stoker, the South African Christian philosopher, goes a step beyond Brunner and pointedly relates justice to the status which God has given men and women in the creation.

God's Word revelation sheds an even keener light on the status of man. Viewed in its divine context and in religious perspective we note the following concerning man's status. Man alone is created as God's image. Man has been given a calling which he must fulfill, for which he is responsible and for which he must give an account. Man has an *appointment*. He has been appointed as *mandator dei*, as a creaturely viceger-ent of God to act as ruler within the cosmos in the name of the Lord. He has been appointed as ambassador of the Most High. And as such he is entrusted with an *office* to contribute, as a creaturely means in the hands of God, to the realization of God's council and plan in and with the cosmos. In all this man is responsible to God. In other words, with reference to all this, including the function and purpose of his status, man has been given a special *mandate*. He is called to be a child of the King and in his royal status he is at the same time a servant of God. All of this is characteristic of his appointment and the mandate that goes with it, presented to him as man. Must we not find human justice and law here, that is, human rights, legal norms and the legal order?[4]

In this light one can say that *human beings have a right to fulfill the calling God gives them*. All creatures are God's servants (Psalm 119:91). Every creature has a right to be servant of God, to fulfill its particular office for His glory. In the most fundamental link between creatures and Creator—which is the link of the covenant[5]—the Creator speaks His Word and the creature is called upon to do that Word.[6] Creatures have the right to do the words of God. Here the correlation between rights and duties is clear. Creatures differ, and thus their respective rights, because God made them "after their kind." He addresses differing words to them; their callings and offices are thus distinct. The entire creation story in the book of Genesis is filled with a description of callings, of divine assignments. God set the sun and the moon in the firmament of the heavens, the greater light to rule the day and the lesser light to rule the night. He created plants to yield seed and fruit trees to bear fruit upon the earth in order to feed mankind. And he created mankind, male and female, to till and keep the garden of Eden, to fill the earth and subdue it, to love God above all and neighbor as self. Indeed, the very meaning of creatureliness lies in service, in being subject to divine ordinances which are the pointers to blessing, shalom, the life that is good. Creatures have the *right* to perform these divine assignments. They have a right to the institutions and the resources needed to carry them out.

The legal framework in a society like ours consists fundamentally of three types of rights—the rights of persons, of institutions and associations, and of the state. First, personal rights. The norm of justice requires a social order in which men and women can express themselves as God's imagers. To put it another way, justice requires social space for human personality. By personality I mean the human self whose calling lies in love of God and love of fellowman. It is at this point that one can again see clearly the correlation between rights and duties. The duty to love God is ineradicable from the covenantal bond between God and humans; sin does not eliminate that duty. At the same time, the right to love God is inalienable. We cannot surrender it because it defines our very existence, our humanness, our creatureliness as male and female.

In the revelation of Christ, the Word made flesh, we know what love is. But at this point we are also confronted with what is perhaps the most difficult problem in the history of human rights. Because of sin, the gods men love are many, and for centuries the lovers of God have denied the right of others to love their god. If *in Christ* we know what it means to love God, do persons who claim to love God as revealed by Buddha or Mohammed have a right to the fulfillment of their claim? And what about persons who claim that the god they are called upon to love is human personality itself? A just society may not discriminate between one religion and another. The wheat and the tares are allowed to coexist until *God's* final day of judgment. This does not mean that the social order is neutral with respect to religions. Societal orders ought to be so structured that a multiplicity of religions can flourish side by side. This will be of increasing import when we will see a rapid growth of interchange among the world's civilizations and cultures. Religion is the prime factor not only in the value systems of persons but also in the fabric of cultures and civilizations. If the society of the future will be one of peace and justice, it must be one where the right to freedom of religion is accorded preeminence, where there are no laws "respecting an establishment of religion, or prohibiting the free exercise thereof." (First Amendment, U.S. Constitution)

The rights of persons to fulfill their callings implies *the right to be,* the right to life itself, the right to be unharmed. Again we are reminded of our dependence on the Roman law.

> *Iuris praecepta sunt haec: honeste vivere, alterum non laedere, suum cuique tribuere.*[7]

> The precepts of law are these: to live honestly, not to harm another, to render to each his due.

This right to be is not merely that of the human species. It belongs to every individual human life, from the beginning of its existence at conception to its end at death. Human life on earth always exists in bodies of flesh and blood and bones. These individual bodies have a right to remain whole, not to be harmed, aborted, maimed, tortured, molested, placed in hostage, terrorized. The basic needs of individual bodies to food, nurture, shelter and care are implicit in the right to life. The biblical message pointedly indicates that the fulfillment of such needs is not a matter of charity but of justice, and is therefore a matter of the structure of the public order. Justice requires such an allocation of material and cultural goods that human life is made possible, is protected, enhanced, and enabled to carry on a multiplicity of tasks in history. The building of cultures and societies entails the use of "nature" and its resources. Again, this is not a right of the human species or the human community. The earth is the Lord's; and *persons* have the right to a stewardly possession and use of it. In this sense, the right to private property is as essential as the right to privacy in a developed, highly differentiated society like ours.[8]

The second category of rights is that of institutions. I employ the word "institution" here in a specific sense to refer to communities and associations of which persons are members. Typical communities are marriages, families, churches and states. Associations are generally dependent upon the principle of voluntary joining and leaving on the part of their members.[9] These include schools, universities, industrial enterprises, philanthropic and artistic organizations, political parties, labor unions, social clubs, the media, and the hundreds of freely established associations characteristic of modern democratic societies.

Communities and associations have an identity that is directly dependent upon their office, the service they render society. Their rights are correlative with their office. The right of an institution is its authority to make legally binding decisions for its members pertinent to its office.[10] A society is genuinely free when both persons and institutions can exercise their rights in this sense, without interference by external powers. With reference to the question of the impact of law on religious expression and freedom, we have to address the issue of whether religious freedom is primarily a matter of personal rights and the right of churches or whether that freedom is also essential for non-church institutions. But first let's consider the third category of rights—those of the state. Since the state is also an institution, its rights do not in principle need separate attention. However, since the impact of *its* "law" on religious freedom is our focus, practical considerations justify this in the present context. The state has rights peculiar to it because it has a unique office. That office is of divine origin: it is God's servant for our good. (Cf. Romans 13:4.) Its distinctive office is to establish and maintain a public realm in which the rights of persons and institutions are recognized, protected, and guaranteed. The state does not create these rights; instead, it must acknowledge divinely sanctioned and given rights, and establish spheres of freedom within which persons and institutions can exercise rights for the fulfillment of their respective offices, callings, and responsibilities.

The "good" which the state is called upon to establish is the *salus publica,* the public good. This has a variety of implications. In the first place, it means that the state's administration of justice must protect each person within its realm, irrespective of belief, race, class, or sex. Each person must be deemed equal before the law of the land. In the second place, the state is a public institution in that its membership—citizenship—must be open to everyone born within its borders. Under no circumstances is the state allowed to annul the citizenship of its members. In the third place, the state is public in that the legal order which it establishes ought to be one in which the spheres of freedom for the nonpolitical institutions and associations are guaranteed and protected from external interference. It must do that in such a way that no person or institution exploits, usurps, or abuses another. The state is called upon to guarantee peace for the commonwealth so that communities and associations domiciled within its territory can develop the "inner law of their being," the specific mandate for which the Creator called them into being through the historical deeds of men and women in time. In the fourth place, the state is a public institution because it has the calling—with other states—to establish an international framework of law which maintains peace and justice among nations and among multinational powers. Finally, states are public because they have the right to exercise "the power of the sword" within the entire territory over which their jurisdiction extends. Only states can have a monopoly of that power; as soon as they lose that monopoly they cease to be states. Though that power is immense, it is limited both in kind ("sword") and in use (public justice). Acquisition of different kinds of power results in tyranny at home and imperialism abroad.

Along with the biblical setting and the legal framework, we must also consider the constitutional structure. After all, when we speak of the impact of *law* on religious expression and freedom, we are in the final analysis speaking of *constitutional law* because legislative stipulations and administrative regulations affecting religion will, if challenged, have to pass the test of constitutionality.

A constitution is the body of fundamental rules which determines "the exercise of the sovereign power in the state"[11] and guarantees certain rights to the people. Two questions must be distinguished here. First, does the U.S. Constitution contain provisions which adequately protect the people's rights of religious expression and freedom? Second, has the U.S. Supreme Court properly interpreted these provisions? I will focus primarily on the first question because, in my view, the public debate concerning it leaves a great deal to be desired.

We are not in the habit of critiquing the provisions of the Constitution because we stand in awe of this document. And rightly so. The Constitution, along with the English Bill of Rights of 1689 and the French Declaration of the Rights of Man and of the Citizen of 1789, is one of the most significant and influential political documents of the modern age. The Constitution has withstood the test of time. Though formulated by representatives from thirteen thinly populated former colonies of diverse cultural and religious leanings, it provided the base for 200 years of development of the United States into the most powerful nation on earth. It was one of the most formative powers that kept this body politic together and could, at times of crisis, be amended to meet new needs. A political document of such stature has an aura of invincible splendor that humbles the student of constitutional law.

Moreover, the clauses affecting religion in the First Amendment—"Congress shall make no law respecting an establishment of religion, or prohibiting the free exercise thereof"—have exercised a benignant impact on American society. The establishment clause prevented the legal primacy of any denomination so that the equality of each citizen before the law became a reality, at least from a formal point of view. The fact that membership in the traditional Anglo-Saxon denominations carried with it definite social, economic and even political advantages must be attributed more to the cultural moorings of American civilization than to its legal structure. And the free exercise clause eliminated potential legal obstacles in the way of the stunning diversity of ecclesiastical life in the United States—a diversity unique in the modern age.

Nonetheless, these outstanding features of the Constitution should not blind us to its shortcomings that today not only contribute to confusion in the relation between religion and the public realm but also hinder the proper expression of religious freedom in American society. These shortcomings are related to the biblical underpinnings of human rights and the threefold societal diversity of rights.

The Constitution is an embodiment of the eighteenth-century Enlightenment in its moderate form.[12] The Enlightenment marked the unfolding of humanism, the religion which idolizes the self-realization of human personality. In its radicality, humanism views the autonomy of the human will as the final source of "values" for ethics. Since the eighteenth century, humanism considered technical rationality in science as the most fitting instrument in extracting nature's resources in industrial production. And humanism, in its late bourgeois phase, viewed the acquisition of material abundance for our bodily needs as the goal of progressive history.[13] Humanism is the post-Christian religion of the West. In its most radical forms it *negates* the relevance of God's existence, the light of biblical revelation, the created structure of natural and social entities, the spiritual essence of human nature, the openness of human beings toward God, and the rootedness of cultural traditions and social institutions in the Christian foundations of Western civilization. Humanism is a secularized version of the Christian religion: it places the transcendent spiritual realities of the Christian faith within the confines of an immanent historical process subject to the control of the autonomous human will.[14]

Immanentized spiritual movements as a rule express themselves historically in three dialectically interrelated ways: radicalism, moderation, conservatism. (The political movements that parallel these expressions are generally referred to as the left, the center, and the right.) In the modern age, France was the center of radicalism, England of moderation, and Germany of conservatism. Moderate humanism took into consideration the importance of continuity in cultural and social change, and it accommodated itself politically to the Christian religion by making the public realm secular and by confining religion to the private spheres of home and church. John Locke (1632-1704) was the political philosopher who most clearly articulated the political accommodation between the Christian religion and modern, individualist humanism. Because of Locke's influence on the Founding Fathers, it is essential that we understand his position on the relation between religion and society. One doesn't have to deny Locke's personal commitment as a Christian to be aware of his basic post-Christian stance in sociopolitical matters which he shared with Thomas Hobbes.

> Both men began with a common point of departure, the assumption that man is a product of his experience and that his nature is rooted in material reality rather than in divine

ordination. The assumption was revolutionary; it swept away
the belief in providence that underlay medieval society and
instead pointed to man's potential for ordering society as he
saw fit.[15]

In distinction from Hobbes, the radical, Locke searched
for a moderate political accommodation with the Christian
religion. He did this perhaps most clearly in *A Letter Concerning Toleration,* published in 1689. Here Locke first presents his view of the state. It is a radically secular, even
materialist conception. It is best to quote his own words.

> The commonwealth seems to me to be a society of men
> constituted only for the procuring, preserving, and advancing
> of their own civil interests.
> Civil interests I call life, liberty, health and indolency of
> body; and the possession of outward things, such as money,
> lands, houses, furniture, and the like.
> It is the duty of the civil magistrate, by the impartial execu-
> tion of equal laws, to secure unto all the people in general, and
> to every one of his subjects in particular, the just possession of
> these things belonging to this life.[16]

After thus reducing the scope of government to "secular
interests"[17] which in effect amounts to "the preservation
of property,"[18] Locke defines the church.

> A church, then, I take to be a voluntary society of men,
> joining themselves together of their own accord in order to
> the public worshiping of God in such manner as they judge
> acceptable to Him, and effectual to the salvation of their
> souls.[19]

After this speedy reduction of religion to the pursuit of
soul salvation, Locke turns to the question of the relation
between state and church. He makes two points. "The
only business of the church is the salvation of souls, and it
no ways concerns the commonwealth."[20] But he is aware
that in certain circumstances the interests of the church
may collide with the interests of the state. In that case the

church must give in to the state. "But those things that are prejudicial to the commonweal of a people in their ordinary use, and are therefore forbidden by laws, those things ought not to be permitted to churches in their sacred rights."[21]

With this defense of toleration, Locke in effect provided the basis for secular society in its moderate, liberal form. This basis comprised several elements, two of which are indispensable: first, the state is secular, governed by the rational consent of the governed; and second, religion is a matter of the salvation of the soul, best achieved in the church of one's choice. The First Amendment of the Constitution embodies these principles. The establishment clause severs the link between the state and church, and, in an ever increasing manner, the link between the state and religion. Further, the free exercise clause guarantees the individual's religious freedom in whatever church he seeks to express it.

There is one additional complication. The conception of society, both in Locke and in the Founding Fathers, was individualistic. This meant that societal relationships were viewed in terms of the wills of the individual persons comprising these relationships. In the realm of law, it meant that the rights of individuals are protected in the Bill of Rights while the rights of communities and associations are not mentioned except indirectly in the Third Amendment, where the privacy of the family is protected ("No Soldier shall, in time of peace be quartered in any house, without the consent of the Owner. . .").

With this background, it should come as no surprise that with reference to the expression of religious freedom we are in a constitutional bind. The two centuries of American history have witnessed an amazing proliferation of communities and associations in the form of churches, schools, colleges, universities, industries, labor unions, charitable organizations, and, especially in recent decades,

caring institutions for the very young and the very old, for
the disabled and the handicapped. The expression of religious freedom is guaranteed in the churches. But it is of
the very nature of religion to express itself also in these
"mediating structures"[22] that fill society between the individual and the state. Precisely because they are mediating
structures, they inevitably have links with individuals,
who are their members, and with the state, which must
acknowledge, protect and guarantee the rights peculiar to
their nature, identity, and office. These mediating structures are established by ordinary people for a great variety
of reasons—profits of money, pleasures of the body, and
praise of God. I suspect that the latter reason is still fore-
most. How then can we have a free society when the rights
of the mediating structures organized for the praise of God
are not constitutionally protected? From the schools parents expect for their children an education that is in tune
with their basic world view. From the colleges and universities we expect the development of the mind. From the
caring institutions we expect legal adoption arrangement
for children, medical care for the sick, assistance for the
physically and mentally disabled, protection for the elder-
ly. These concerns overlap with those of the state. But
does this overlap mean that the religious character of these
mediating structures must be eradicated as soon as the state
becomes involved, especially when public funds are used?
If that is the meaning of the establishment clause, its effect
is "the establishment of a religion of secularism," as Justice
Potter Stewart hinted in his dissent in the *Schempp* case.[23]
The U.S. Supreme Court has indeed interpreted the establishment clause in this way, especially since the *Everson*
case.[24] In view of this, we are today faced with the compelling need for "Disestablishment a Second Time."[25]

The disestablishment we need today is not a severing of
the link between the state and its established church, as in
the eighteenth century, but rather a severing of the links

between the state and the secularism established and imposed in mediating structures that are closely connected with the state, especially in the areas of health, education, and welfare. I am not advocating a universal severance of the links between the state and the mediating structures operating in these areas. I am not advocating a medical, educational, or social laissez-faire policy (although a cutting back of governmental bureaucracy and an increase in personal and institutional responsibilities in these areas ought to be welcomed). Nor am I advocating a states' rights solution to these problems (as if local and state governments are inherently less secular than the federal government). The solution I am advocating is *the disestablishment of secularism* in the mediating structures on the part of every level of government and *the equal protection of the free exercise of religion* in these structures. In the area of education, for example, governments are legitimately involved because without education citizens cannot assume political responsibilities in a democracy. But parents are equally interested in education. The interests of the government and the interests of the parents can be met in a system of governmentally certified and funded schools religiously differentiated according to the religious convictions of the parents whether they be secular, Jewish, or Christian. Similar solutions are possible in the areas of health and welfare.

I am aware that what I am advocating involves a fundamental restructuring of the American legal system. I dare to defend this proposition since I am convinced that the establishment of secularism is a tyranny that prohibits free exercise of both personal and institutional rights.

Does a restructuring of the legal system require constitutional reform? I would like to answer this question first by pointing out that there is a major example of juridical reflection that better covers this area than the U.S. Constitution, and secondly, by suggesting that the U.S. Constitution can serve as the legal basis for expanding the free exercise of both personal and institutional rights. The documents to which I refer are the Charter of the United Nations adopted on June 26, 1945, and the Universal Declaration of Human Rights, drafted by the United Nations Commission on Human Rights under the chairpersonship of Eleanor Roosevelt and adopted by the General Assembly on December 10, 1948. The Charter sets out the internal structure of the United Nations; the Declaration is in effect a universal Bill of Rights. This Declaration is a document born within the civilization of the West, revealing the impact of both humanism and Christianity. It displays many weaknesses, but it is the most adequate statement of rights the civilized world has formulated, even if it has not managed to live up to its demands. It is important because it has gone beyond the individualism of the Enlightenment world view reflected in the U.S. Bill of Rights. The personal rights recognized in the U.S. Bill of Rights are incorporated in the Declaration, but in addition there is a surprising list of institutional rights which has not received the attention it deserves. Here are the relevant articles.

Article 16. 1. Men and women of full age, without any limitation due to race, nationality or religion, have the right to marry and to found a family. . . .

3. The family is the natural and fundamental group unit of society and is entitled to protection by society and the State.

Article 18. Everyone has the right to freedom of thought, conscience and religion; this right includes freedom to change his religion or belief, and freedom, either alone or in community with others and in public or private, to manifest his religion in teaching, practice, worship and observance.

Article 20. 1. Everyone has the right to freedom of peaceful assembly and association.

2. No one may be compelled to belong to an association.

Article 26. 1. Everyone has the right to education. Education shall be free, at least in the elementary and fundamental stages. Elementary education shall be compulsory. . . .

3. Parents have a prior right to choose the kind of education that shall be given to their children.

Article 29. 1. Everyone has duties to the community in which alone the free and full development of his personality is possible.

2. In the exercise of his rights and freedoms, everyone shall be subject only to such limitations as are determined by law solely for the purpose of securing due recognition and respect for the rights and freedoms of others and of meeting the just requirements of morality, public order and the general welfare in a democratic society.

As its Preamble states, the Universal Declaration of Human Rights was proclaimed by the General Assembly of the United Nations "as a common standard of achievement for all people and nations." It is not binding law in any state, but serves as an excellent model for constitutional reform because it recognizes the rights of such institutions as marriage and family, the freedom of association (including the indispensable corollary—the freedom *not* to belong to an association), and the freedom without distinction of any kind to manifest one's belief, either alone or in community.

It is singularly unfortunate that Canada, which is going through the most significant constitutional reform in its entire history, has not benefited from the common standard contained in the Universal Declaration. The Canadian Charter of Rights and Freedoms, which is Part I of the proposed Constitution, declares the following Fundamental Freedoms in article 2:

freedom of conscience and religion

freedom of thought, belief, opinion and expression, including freedom of the press and other media of communication freedom of peaceful assembly

freedom of association[26]

There is little here that goes beyond the First Amendment of the U.S. Constitution, and one can therefore predict that in fifty years the Supreme Court of Canada will be entangled in a legal labyrinth with respect to the religious rights of the mediating structures as confusing as the chaos we now face in the United States.[27]

The United States is not going through a period of constitutional reform, and amendments do not readily receive the required support, as the history of both the proposed Equal Rights Amendment and the Anti-Abortion Amendment shows. How then can the disestablishment of secularism be legally achieved? How can the free exercise of religion without discrimination in the health, education, and welfare institutions be guaranteed? I believe that within the present constitutional framework there are three available avenues. First, there is ample historical evidence that the establishment clause was included in the First Amendment to disestablish churches.[28] The question of religious freedom *in schools* is not properly a matter of the establishment clause (except when the state uses schools to establish the religion it prefers). Constitutional lawyers should argue this strict interpretation of the clause.

In the second place, the nature, content and scope of religion is not defined in the First Amendment.[29] The rights pertinent to the free exercise thereof can only be defined by its adherents, and the exercise of these rights should not be prohibited unless such exercise conflicts with the legitimate demands of the public realm itself. (For example, the refusal of parents, on religious grounds, to permit the administration of blood transfusion to save the life of their child would—in my view—constitute an offense against the public realm.) In recent decades the Supreme Court has begun to acknowledge that the free exercise of religion cannot possibly be confined to personal belief and ecclesiastical practice. It has protected the free exercise of religion even when this collided with the interests of the state, as in the conscientious objectors cases.[30] Constitutional lawyers will have to pursue this argument further, to extend to the expression of religious freedoms in the various spheres outside of the church. The Constitution itself does not prohibit such an extension.

In the third place, there are three amendments to the Constitution whose provisions can be properly used to defend a relation between religion and the state radically different from the "absolute separation" imposed on American society by the Supreme Court on the basis of a misinterpretation of the establishment clause. The Fourteenth Amendment, in part, reads as follows: "No State shall make or enforce any law which shall abridge the privileges or immunities of citizens of the United States; nor shall any State deprive any person of life, liberty, or property, without due process of law; nor deny to any person within its jurisdiction the equal protection of the laws." In my view, any state which funds secular public schools while refusing to fund independent private schools abridges the privileges of the citizens who support the private schools, deprives them of property without due process, and denies them the equal protection of the laws. The same argument holds for similar discrimination in the areas of health and welfare.

And then there is the Tenth Amendment: "The powers not delegated to the United States by the Constitution, nor prohibited by it to the States, are reserved to the States respectively, or to the people." The Founding Fathers established a nontotalitarian state. This means that the state does not have a monopoly of power in society. Other sectors have powers of their own. We acknowledge a plurality of power when we defend free enterprise in the economic sector. There is no constitutional prohibition of a defense of a plurality of power in the cultural sectors, whose powers today are increasingly absorbed into the political system.

Finally, the Ninth Amendment reads: "The enumeration in the Constitution of certain rights, shall not be construed to deny or disparage others retained by the people." The rights of the people to the free exercise of religion in the nonchurch spheres of society are today both denied and disparaged. As a rule, rights have to be fought for; they don't come on a golden platter. The Ninth Amendment provides a constitutional base for this battle.

By suggesting that religious rights should be dealt with in the light of these three amendments I am really saying that the future battle should be fought much more in terms of *rights,* which the courts are called upon to defend, rather than in terms of *religion,* which the courts are not legally competent to define. The disestablishment of the religion of secularism must be achieved by getting the combatants out of the prison of the Supreme Court's interpretation of the First Amendment's establishment clause, which is largely irrelevant to the issues at stake. The establishment clause cut America off from the Constantinian entanglement of church and state, and did so properly. The Bill of Rights *as a whole* laid the basis for a free society, including the expression of the rights of religion. Let's then bring the entire Bill of Rights into the picture!

At the beginning of the modern era the societies of western Europe were torn by the wars of religion. The colonies along the eastern seaboard and later the independent United States were havens for those driven from their homelands because of religious persecution. The Constitution established channels for a society of toleration. Today we realize that these channels are partly blocked because secularism has become the religion of the public realm. The establishment of this religion brings with it both injustice and discrimination, and thus the danger for new wars of religion, undoubtedly fought with different weapons. This danger can be averted. Let us openly and honestly recognize that the American citizenry is religiously divided. And then let us avail ourselves of the constitutional weapons so that the legitimate rights of each religious segment in the citizenry are properly acknowledged, not only in the private spheres of life but also in the public realm.

NOTES

[1]Aristotle, *The Politics of Aristotle,* translated by Ernest Barker (London: Oxford University Press, 1946), p. 65n.

[2]Here it should be kept in mind that the Bible presents a fundamental antithesis between the sin of mankind and the work of God in creation and redemption. It does not present an antithesis between creation and redemption. Redemption is the restoration of creation by divine grace. Christian world views which proceed from the (relative) autonomy of creation lead to a natural law conception of justice, dominant in classical Roman Catholic thought. See John Courtney Murray, *We Hold These Truths: Catholic Reflections on the American Proposition* (New York: Sheed & Ward, 1960); and its Protestant parallel, Carl F.H. Henry, *Aspects of Christian Social Ethics* (Grand Rapids: Eerdmans, 1964). Christian world views which (tend to) isolate redemption from creation lead to a Christomonistic conception of justice. Because of the eclipse of the doctrine of creation in modern Christian thought, such Christomonistic conceptions are dominant. See Karl Barth, *Community, State and Church* (New York: Doubleday, 1960); Jacques Ellul, *Le fondement théologique du droit* (1946); and John Howard Yoder, *The Christian Witness to the State* (Newton, Kansas: Faith and Life Press, 1964). Finally, Christian world views that take as their point of departure the fall into sin tend to reject the inherent goodness of creation and perceive redemption as entirely innovative, often implying the elimination of the existing (sinful) order. In certain types of dispensationalism—made popular by the writings of Hal Lindsey—this annihilation of the existing order will occur when Christ returns in the eschaton. In certain types of liberation theology, Christians are called upon to engage in the destruction of the sinful, existing capitalist order. See José Miranda, *Marx and the Bible: A Critique of the Philosophy of Oppression* (Maryknoll: Orbis Books, 1974). These various Christian world views have their counterparts in post-Christian secular thought, such as modern natural law, Marxism, and the radical wing of the counterculture from Rousseau to Roszak.

[3]Emil Brunner, *Justice and the Social Order* (New York, 1945), p. 83.

[4]H. G. Stoker, *Die aard en die rol van die req* [The Nature and Role of Law] (Johannesburg, 1970), p. 15. My own translation.

[5]For a treatment of the history of biblical revelation in the light of the covenant, see S. G. de Graaf, *Promise and Deliverance*, 4 vols. (St. Catherines, Ontario: Paideia, 1977 *seq.*), and H. E. Runner's "Translator's Introduction" to vol. 3, pp. 11-21.

[6]Cf. Bernard Zylstra, "Thy Word Our Life," in James H. Olthuis, *et al., Will All The King's Men?* (Toronto: Wedge, 1972), pp. 153-221.

[7]Justinian, *Institutiones* I.1.3.

[8]Cf. Hannah Arendt, *Crises of the Republic* (New York: Harcourt Brace Jovanovich, 1972), pp. 211f.

[9]Herman Dooyeweerd's sociological distinctions of the various kinds of human relations in a differentiated society are helpful. For a quick survey, see L. Kalsbeek, *Contours of a Christian Philosophy: An Introduction to Herman Dooyeweerd's Thought* (Toronto: Wedge, 1975), pp. 196-268.

[10]This matter of the authority and rights of institutions outside of the state is being given increasing attention in sociology of law. F. W. Maitland's Introduction to Otto Gierke's *Political Theories of the Middle Age* (Cambridge University Press, 1900, pp. vii-xlv) is a classic statement of the issue by a legal historian. Herman Dooyeweerd's doctrine of sphere sovereignty deals with this question; cf. his *Roots of Western Culture* (Toronto: Wedge, 1979), pp. 40-60. For an introduction to the relevant literature, especially European, see Bernard Zylstra, *From Pluralism to Collectivism: The Development of Harold Laski's Political Thought* (Assen: Van Gorcum, 1968), pp. 206-220; and James W. Skillen, "The Development of Calvinistic Political Theory in The Netherlands, with Particular Reference to the Thought of Herman Dooyeweerd." Ph.D. dissertation, Duke University, 1973. See also H. Evan Runner, "Sphere Sovereignty," in *The Relation of the Bible to Learning* (Toronto: Wedge, second edition, 1981), Lecture V.

[11]Cf. A. V. Dicey, *The Law of the Constitution* (London: MacMillan, 1959), p. 23.

[12]Cf. Henry F. May, *The Enlightenment in America* (New York: Oxford University Press, 1976), p. 96f; Carl Becker, *The Heavenly City of the Eighteenth-Century Philosophers* (New Haven: Yale University Press, 1932); and Hannah Arendt, *On Revolution* (New York: Viking, 1963).

[13]Cf. Bob Goudzwaard, *Capitalism and Progress* (Toronto: Wedge; Grand Rapids: Eerdmans, 1979), especially Part One.

[14]For a more extensive discussion of the development of secular humanism, see Bernard Zylstra, "Modernity and the American Empire," *International Reformed Bulletin,* first and second quarter, No. 68/69, 1977, pp. 3-19, and the literature cited there.

[15]James Laxer and Robert Laxer, *The Liberal Idea of Canada: Pierre Trudeau and the Question of Canada's Survival* (Toronto: James Lorimer, 1977), p. 80.

[16]John Locke, *A Letter Concerning Toleration* (Indianapolis: Bobbs-Merrill, 1950), p. 17.

[17]*Ibid.*, p. 19.

[18]John Locke, *The Second Treatise of Government* (1690), par. 94.

[19]Locke, *A Letter Concerning Toleration*, p. 20.

[20]*Ibid.*, p. 36.

[21]*Ibid.*, p. 40. Though Francis Schaeffer recognizes that Locke secularized the Christian religion, he nonetheless stresses his dependence on it, especially the Presbyterian tradition. See *How Should We Then Live?* (Old Tappan, New Jersey: Fleming H. Revell, 1976), p. 109.

[22]This term is from Peter Berger. Cf. his essay, "In Praise of Particularity: The Concept of Mediating Structures," in *Facing up to Modernity: Excursions in Society, Politics, and Religion* (New York: Basic Books, 1977), pp. 130-141.

[23]*Abington School District* v. *Schempp*, 374 U.S. 203 (1963) at 226.

[24]*Everson* v. *Board of Education*, 310 U.S. 1 (1947).

[25]See Rockne McCarthy, James W. Skillen, and William A. Harper, *Disestablishment a Second Time: Public Justice for American Schools* (Grand Rapids: Christian University Press). Forthcoming. See also Gordon Spykman, *Society, State, and Schools: A Case for Structural and Confessional Pluralism* (Grand Rapids, Mich.: Eerdmans, 1981).

[26]See "Consolidation of proposed constitutional resolution tabled by the Minister of Justice in the House of Commons on February 13, 1981 with the amendments approved by the House of Commons on April 23, 1981 and by the Senate on April 24, 1981." Issued by the Department of Justice in Ottawa. The amendments to the proposed Constitution for Canada, sent to the British Parliament in November 1981, do not affect the wording of Article 2.

[27]This could have been avoided if the submissions to the constitutional committee of Parliament by Roman Catholic, Mennonite, and relevant Reformed institutions had been paid attention to. See, for instance, the brief presented by the Committee for Justice and Liberty (CJL), a Toronto-based Christian public interest group, to the Special Joint Committee of the Senate and the House of Commons on the Constitution. For an overall assessment, see Paul Marshall, "Reflections on the Constitutional Package," *Catalyst* (publication of the CJL), June 1981, p. 8f.

[28]See Anson Phelps Stokes, *Church and State in the United States*, 3 vols. (New York: Harper, 1950), vol. 1, pp. 64-654.

[29]See Sharon L. Worthing, " 'Religion' and 'Religious Institutions' under the First Amendment," *Pepperdine Law Review*, vol. 7 (1980), pp. 313-354.

[30]See, for instance, *United States* v. *Seeger*, 380 U.S. 163 (1965).

8 CRIMINAL JUSTICE: HOW CAN WE NOT BE INVOLVED?

Charles W. Colson

Instead of asking ourselves how we can be involved in issues of criminal justice, a better question is, How can we *not* be involved? How can we minister to people who are living in filth and despair, see the injustice in prisons and not care? Jesus cared. During His earthly ministry He healed the lame, gave sight to the blind, fed the hungry and preached about going into the prisons, because He cared about the human physical and mental condition as well as the spiritual condition.

The more I read Scripture, the more deeply I am convinced of the need for Christians to come under the authority of Holy Scripture, to accept it as the infallible, inerrant Word of God. When we read Scripture in this way we can more clearly recognize injustice for what it really is and see why it grieves God.

Jeremiah's passion was for justice, and the prophet Amos said, "Yes, remodel your courts to bring justice for the people while there's still time." The entire prophetic tradition of the Old Testament calls people to repentance and to justice. Solomon asked for the ability to know right from wrong and to do justice among God's people. And Jesus came, setting new standards of justice. To the adulteress about to be stoned, Jesus said, "Go and sin no more." For Zacchaeus, the corrupt tax collector, Jesus established a system of restitution.

I'm convinced that none of us can love the Lord our God with all our heart, mind, and soul, and love our neighbor like ourselves, without sharing a passion for human justice. Nowhere in America's society today is the cry for justice louder than in the 600 prisons and penitentiaries of America. And that is where Christians must go to preach the Good News.

We are seeing concern for justice in connection with the free exercise of religious beliefs. All Christians must be interested in this area because ultimately we are all affected. If the state restricts your freedoms, are mine safe? There is, of course, a tension between individual liberty and the good of the whole state. The Constitution and Bill of Rights stand at the points of conflict. When we feel that our rights under those documents are being abridged, it is appropriate to respond.

But our concern for justice cannot end here. Are we really interested in justice if we struggle only for our own rights? Our struggle, our energies, our advocacy must also include those who are denied justice, whoever and wherever they may be.

The reason why Christians should care about criminal justice is that we are ministers of the Good News of Jesus Christ. At Prison Fellowship, we go into prisons to build Christian fellowships. We take teaching teams into prison; we take inmates out. Approximately 600 men and women have come out of prison, participated in discipleship training with us, and then gone back to complete their sentences. Our job is to plant the Church behind prison walls, to encourage and exhort the Church of Jesus Christ to do that which we are biblically commanded to do. So often people will say they understand that the Bible tells us to go into prisons to preach the Good News, but they wonder what that has to do with criminal justice and reform.

On one occasion I arrived at Walla Walla Penitentiary in Washington on the day when the 1400 inmates were being released from a four-month lockdown, which means they had been in their cells that entire time. A guard had been killed several months before, and the warden simply locked the prison down. I spoke in maximum security that day. A week later we returned for a seminar and nine of the inmates asked to meet with the leader, George Soltau. They told him: "Mr. Soltau, at the very time Chuck Colson was speaking last week, we had planned a riot; we were going to kill five guards (retaliation for their brutality during the lockdown), but one of our leaders became a Christian and we listened to you. We believe you're on the level, and we'd like to work with you. We'd like to try to find some solutions in this prison, short of violence. Will you work with us?"

We knew that certain lives were at stake and said yes. Later we were appointed intermediary between the prison population and the prison staff and worked full-time to avert violence, and to mediate disputes. We set up grievance procedures, worked to get an inmate council going. All the while, we preached the Gospel and conducted seminars to which eighty-five black Muslims came. Their lives were changed. Even so, we were like kids running around sticking fingers in the dike to keep the water from pouring in. In the end, I addressed the legislature twice, we worked up some reform legislation, and we met with the governor. Today our reform package is making its way through the Washington State legislature and there's been only one killing in the last year and a half in Walla Walla, a place once noted for violence.

The legal profession, and particularly its Christian

members, must take a hard look at the criminal justice
problem in America today. I believe we're in a cycle, historically. We can look back and see that the great nations
and empires of human history have gone through the same
cycle—first a period of moral decay, when authority is
assaulted and attacked and when there are no absolutes, a
time of materialism and self-gratification, followed by a
rise in lawlessness. We went through that in the '60s.

Lawlessness is countered in either one of two ways: by
repression or with a spiritual awakening. Hitler came to
power by promising law and order and to clean up the
streets of Germany. He was popular and was supported by
much of the liberal church.

On the other hand, the spiritual awakening of the Wes-
ley-Wilberforce era, that great campaign to abolish slavery, saved England. God's people cared. They not only
preached the Good News as Wesley did, but also worked
for human justice as Wilberforce and the Clapham sect did
in the Parliament and throughout the power structure of
England.

And that's our choice today—repression or a spiritual
awakening—in a year when one out of three American
homes will be directly affected by crime. It's a crisis.
Already we're seeing signs of repression. A senator has
announced that he would propose the death penalty not
only for assassination of a president, but for attempted
assassination as well. From there it could extend to judges,
congressmen and other public officials, and from attempted assassination to conspiracy and then to political dissent.
It's an inevitable consequence when one out of three
American households are being touched by crime.

Recent polls show that crime has replaced inflation as
the number one domestic concern of Americans. The rate
of violent crime alone rose a staggering thirteen percent
last year. The public says to get tough, and I can't blame
them. The problem is that the public doesn't understand

the problem, basically because of apathy. As one sociologist has pointed out, we follow the toilet assumption in America. If we have problems, we flush them down the toilet, thinking everything is fine because it's out of sight. That's what we do with our institutions—we take the unwanted human beings and flush them down the toilet until the sewer system backs up. And right now the sewer system is backed up in the American criminal justice system. Getting tough may have been the problem rather than the solution. The average sentence in the federal judiciary has gone from 16.5 months in 1945 to 45.2 months in 1975. We incarcerate in the United States of America more people—240 per 100,000—than any other nation except the Soviet Union and South Africa. We have 350,000 men and women in the pits and dungeons we call prison.

What are prisons for? They started as a Christian reform, almost 200 years ago. The Quakers took the Walnut Street Jail in Philadelphia and turned it into a place where penitents could go—hence the name penitentiary. It was to be a humane reform so that we would no longer put people in stocks or beat them, but instead we would put them into a solitary cell where they could repent before God, be cleansed, and come out rehabilitated. Instead, they came out insane. But by then it had become a modern reform. In 1790 New York adopted it as the primary form of punishment; every state followed, and eventually all of the Western world. The record shows 200 years of absolute failure.

If prisons worked, we wouldn't have a crime rate soaring out of control in the United States. If prisons deterred crime, they wouldn't be full and overflowing. The crime rate wouldn't be going up faster here than anywhere in the world. In Holland, where the prison population has been reduced the crime rate is coming down. In England, where most of the non-violent offenders are taken out of prison and put into service or work projects in the communities, the crime rate has started coming down steadily. In Minnesota, which has the second lowest per capita incarceration rate for non-violent offenders, the prison population has been declining at a time when it's going up in every other state. Some believe that we incarcerate more people in America because we have more crime. I think it is an equally valid possibility that we have more crime in America because we incarcerate more people.

Of course, there are no easy solutions to the problems of crime and punishment, but I am absolutely positive that what we're now doing is not working. Just to give you an idea of the enormity of the problem, we have $5.6 billion in new prison construction on the books in America today. That is slightly larger than the Federal Highway program was when it began in 1956. I recently visited with five governors, four of whom told me that they will bankrupt their states if they have to build the number of prison cells required under the present sentencing structures in each of their states. In Indiana, $200 million in new prison construction is planned. Minnesota has just built a prison at a cost of $32.5 million. That's $80,000 per bed, but they can't open the prison because there was a shortfall of revenues. They don't have the money; there's no lending authority, they can't borrow, they can't go into deficit financing, and it will cost $30,000 per year per inmate to operate the new prison. The governor said, "There's nothing we can do. We're not going to open the prison. We can't afford to run it."

We must come up with constructive alternatives. The legal profession must be a source—a force in our community—that creates a public attitude that will permit responsible politicians to make decisions before it's too late.

Christian lawyers can do some things to bring sense into the debate on crime, violence, justice and prisons in America. We have to do it quickly. The public is not going to allow much more time to elapse before they will insist upon solutions which may create further injustice in our system. For example, when I first went to the White House, we had power over the District of Columbia. The crime rate was so high in the District of Columbia the mayor was given orders and money to hire twice as many police. He did. The crime rate went up thirty-one percent the next year. The D.C. police force was increased another twenty percent and the crime rate went up thirty percent.

I am convinced that we simply don't have the resources in society to isolate all the potential offenders. Our hope is to find other ways to deal with the wrong moral choices that human beings make within our society. We know, for example, one of those ways is restitution. Where restitution programs have been tried as an alternative to incarceration, they have been enormously successful. It won't take care of all the cases, but it's better than what we are doing: better than spending $17,000 a year to incarcerate a person, particularly a nonviolent person, in a violent place called prison. Restitution has been tried in a number of places in a variety of ways. There are other reforms, such as community service, which the British are using with great effect. We could use sentence review in the states. Disparity of sentencing is the chief cause of bitterness in American prisons today. I found a fellow doing four to twenty-five years for stealing $10 worth of beer from his neighbor's garage. He was put into an Ohio State penitentiary where in the first week he was assaulted several times. His parents paid back the beer and it has been established before the judge that he was an alcoholic. The judge, nonetheless, said, "It's your third offense, I'm giving you four to twenty-five years." We must stop putting kids like that into penitentiaries where they are raped and beaten, where they learn to use a knife to survive, where they lie, cheat, steal, and keep quiet in order not to get their throats slit. We put them into that kind of an environment and expect them to behave when they get out. It's preposterous. We should take kids like that and put them out working on the fire engine in the firehouse, or doing community clean-up jobs, or something else constructive.

I ran the washing machine and did the prison laundry in Maxwell Prison in Montgomery, Alabama. The fellow next to me who ran the dryer was the former Chairman of the Board of the American Medical Association. He had been convicted of a stock fraud in a bank in which he had served on the Board of Directors. It had nothing to do with practicing medicine. The doctor would run the dryer, I'd run the washer; some days I'd run the dryer and he'd run the washer, just for variety. We had no doctor in that prison, housing 300 men. Several times during the year and a half the doctor was in prison, he asked if he could practice medicine as a way of serving his sentence. The answer was, no; it was against the prison regulations. A prisoner had a heart attack and the doctor couldn't touch him, so the man had to wait for the ambulance to come. Similarly, there were carpenters in that prison. At the same time prison officials were contracting for a company to put an extension on the education wing of the library building, there were carpenters mowing lawns, or sitting on their bunks, doing nothing, day in and day out. It's insanity.

My friend the doctor could have worked in a ghetto area for two, three, four years with no or minimal pay, to help poor people who are without medical care. Instead, they sentenced him to a penitentiary at a cost to taxpayers of $20,000 a year. That's ludicrous, it is wrong public policy, and it is injustice.

I have expressed these alternatives to political leaders in half of the states. Some are instituting changes. A governor who is quietly trying to make some changes said, "I don't care if I'm unelectable. It's time somebody did the right thing in this state. But we're not going to have any publicity. As soon as we do, we'll have the whole state up in arms." Attorneys should work to change that kind of public opinion.

Each state could immediately take a look at the nonviolent percentage of its prison population. Can they be released by the governor? Does he have plenary authority simply to go in and cut short their sentences? Because there was no alternative, this was done in Georgia and Florida. Virginia is looking at this as an option to cut the cost of its prison system. If a prisoner has been in for two or three years, has a nonviolent record, has a perfect institutional record, with only six months yet to serve, he should be let out. The less time he lives in that pit of anger and hate and violence, the better chance he has of making it when he gets out of prison.

In one state's worst prison, seventy-three percent of the prison population is violent. That's a very high percentage, but it means twenty-seven percent isn't. I walked through that place and I could not imagine a nonviolent person staying either alive or nonviolent there. It's the same in state after state. As a Christian, I question the morality of putting a nonviolent person in such a place. There must be punishment—justice is integral to the biblical view of society and the Christian view of life, but it doesn't necessarily mean prison, and it certainly doesn't mean taking a nonviolent person and sentencing him to serve time in violence. I wonder if it were tested legally whether it might not be unconstitutional.

In examining criminal justice we must also focus on the nature of crime itself. What is crime? I have researched every theory scholars have come up with from Lombroso, an Italian who decided that one could tell a criminal by his looks, to the ideas in the early part of this century attributing crime to feeblemindedness and ignorance. Today we know that eighty-five percent of the prison population has average or above average I.Q.'s. In the '30s it was believed that poverty, racism and oppression in society were the causes of crime. Most reformers threw up their hands in despair about prisons because they said, "We first have to do something about the basic condition of our society." And so they decided to deal with poverty. Most people in the last twenty-five to thirty years have believed that to be the case, but it's a dangerous myth.

Samenow and Yokelson, two Jewish doctors, one a psychiatrist, one a psychologist, did a seventeen-year study of the causes of crime in America. They started out with a bias that crime is caused by poverty. After 8,000 hours of clinical testing, they produced two massive volumes in which they concluded that based on accumulated evidence, poverty is not the cause of crime, racism is not the cause of crime, oppression is not the cause of crime. All of these may have something to do with crime, but the cause, basically, is the deliberate decision of the wrongdoer to commit evil rather than good. And the answer to crime, therefore, is the conversion of the wrongdoer to a more responsible lifestyle.

That's an extraordinary finding. There can be no question that poverty, racism and environment contribute, but if we're ever going to get at the cause of crime, we have to be alert to what Supreme Court Chief Justice Warren Burger has pointed out: we are creating a class of people and putting them at war with ourselves because we are placing them in institutions which turn them against us. He is calling for some of the very same reforms that we recommend. He recognizes that crime is the result of moral choice and that, therefore, we must provide answers that deal with the moral dimension. He has also recommended that more religious programs be instituted inside prisons as a way to deal with this moral issue.

I urge Christian lawyers today to think about their role in society, and particularly to give a dimension of leadership that may be lacking on the secular side. Lawyers are often looked upon as more concerned about their own economic interests than they are the general welfare. In this technologically oriented, economically motivated society, the lawyer is the arbitrator of competing economic interests. He decides who gets what share of the pie, which means he tends to become a bureaucrat of our economic system.

If we look back into *Lex Rex,* the writings of Rutherford, we see that the Bible is at the root of our view of law, of right and wrong, and of justice and injustice. Lawyers are heirs to that tradition; we ought not to forfeit it and simply become mercantiled judges and referees. We must be concerned about the basic underlying justice of the legal structure of America. We have to be.

Back at that same prison in Walla Walla, there is a converted motorcycle gang leader, now a Christian leader in the prison. Benny told one of our staff members, "Ask Chuck to get me out of this prison." Al said, "We can't get you out of this prison, you know that. But can we help you, brother? What's wrong?" He said, "I haven't seen my wife in six years. I can take the hell of this prison, but I just can't take not seeing her. She lives in Chicago, here I am in Walla Walla."

Al went back to where he was staying that night and he called a couple who live near Chicago and he told them about the problem. The next night they went to see Benny's wife, a beautiful Christian woman with four kids, who is working at two jobs trying to keep the family together. They had a lovely visit with her. That night my friends couldn't sleep. They're not wealthy people, but the next day they went down and bought a plane ticket, round-trip from Chicago to Spokane and took it to Benny's wife. Two weeks later Benny called one of the directors and said, "Thank you, thank you." His voice choked up. "I never thought anyone cared about me, least of all a white man."

I was in that prison shortly after that. Inmates were

coming up to me from all over that place saying, "Thank you for Prison Fellowship!" The inmate leadership group said we had kept our promises and thirty-five convicts gave us a standing ovation. We could preach in that prison, we could hand out tracts, but neither could witness to the people in that prison more than the reuniting of Benny and his wife. That's not just a witness. That is the Gospel.

We Christians, and particularly those of us blessed with the responsibility of being officers of the court, and with ability to plead and influence others, have a duty to reject the egocentric, materialistic values of our society and to do just what happened inside that prison. We need to care and to get involved—to get our hands dirty, if need be—in the pits of prison or in the halls of legislatures—to bring about reform.

9 ATHEISM AND CHRISTIANITY IN THE SOVIET UNION

Harold J. Berman

When we feel discouraged about our own problems it is comforting to turn our attention to the problems of others, especially if they are our adversaries. Then we can devote our energies to removing the "beam" from their eyes, while treating the obstruction in our own as a mere "mote."

When it becomes painful to face up to our deficiencies—the divisions among us, our lack of a common national purpose, our lack of will and commitment—we try to change the subject. We console ourselves with the thought that things are worse elsewhere, and especially in the Soviet Union. There they lack freedom. If we talk about their deficiency we may be able to forget about our own lack of commitment. We have an abundance of freedom, but on the other hand the Soviet Union has an abundance of commitment, of common purpose and will, an abundance of community spirit, and a strong sense of destiny. The severe restriction of religious freedom in the Soviet Union stems above all from the deep commitment of the

Soviet leadership to atheism as a belief system, and as a militant faith. There are other reasons for Soviet anti-religious policies, but the main one is itself "religious" in a deeper sense of that word than usual. It is the Marxist-Leninist conviction that the belief in God is a dangerous superstition, and that the belief in atheism is an essential part of a scientific world view which is a necessary prerequisite to material and moral progress.

Soviet atheism has deep roots in Russian history. It is also derived from Marxism, which is a characteristically Western philosophy; but whereas for Marx atheism was primarily an intellectual matter, an inference drawn from scientific materialism, for Lenin and his Russian followers atheism was a militant faith, a revolt against God. Lenin could have repeated what the Russian revolutionary Bakunin had said, "If God really existed, He would have to be destroyed." This was not the sentimental sort of atheism that is widespread in America today, especially in universities. On the contrary, Leninist atheism is something to be actively believed in, something to be practiced in one's daily life. It rests in part on Marxian intellectual premises: that the ultimate reality is matter, that man's material conditions and needs ultimately determine his conduct and his beliefs, that the basic fact of human history is the struggle to master these material conditions and needs, and that the natural laws of this struggle lead ultimately to Communism. It rests also on the passionate belief—of which Lenin, not Marx, was the great apostle, and which is more Russian than Western—that man is master of his own destiny and by his own power can construct a paradise on earth. It was Lenin, not Marx, who conceived and created the Communist Party as a dedicated elite vanguard, imbued with "social consciousness," whose mission was to lead mankind into that paradise. For Lenin and the Russian Communist Party, atheism represented man's power to replace God, that is, to do by himself, by his intellect and his will, through collective action, what Christianity—and especially Russian Christianity—had taught that only God can do; namely, create a universal peace in the hearts of men.

Many say that "ideology" is no longer a vital factor in Soviet life, that the Soviet people do not really believe in the Marxian theories upon which the Bolshevik Revolution was based. That may be true, just as it may be true that the American people no longer believe in the Jeffersonian theories of agrarian democracy and individual self-reliance which played such a large part in making the American Revolution. But that does not mean that the Soviets—or we—believe in nothing. What they (and we) believe in are watered-down versions of original revolutionary teachings. No doubt Soviet leaders have lost their excessive optimism about the future, and with it, their excessive pessimism about the past. Their beliefs have become less apocalyptic, less militant, more tired. Nevertheless, they still accept large parts of the Leninist world view. Leninist atheism, at least, is still a powerful dogma in the Soviet Communist Party, and the Party's campaign against religion is, if anything, stronger than ever.

Unless we see the issue of Communism versus Religion in the Soviet Union, and especially atheism versus Christianity, as a struggle between two all-embracing, universal faiths, a struggle for the minds and hearts of the Soviet people, we shall be led into serious distortions and over-simplifications concerning Soviet policies. We may think in terms of the traditional struggles between Church and state as we have known them in Western history. We shall see only persecutions of the clergy and prohibitions of religious worship. We shall suppose that the Church in Russia has been forced underground. The truth is that tens of millions of Russians openly attend Church services. And while there have been systematic closings of churches and oppression of the clergy, these are not the most significant features of the Soviet struggle against religion; for it is not the churches as such that the Soviet Party leaders or the Soviet people are primarily concerned about, not "organized religion," but religious belief itself.

In pursuing its goal of creating a society dedicated to material and moral progress, as understood in a Marxist-Leninist perspective, the Communist Party of the Soviet Union has for more than sixty years conducted the most massive assault upon Christianity that the Church has experienced since Roman times. I am not speaking primarily of a physical assault or of the closing of churches, although that is part of it. I am speaking of a systematic campaign to remove traditional religious belief from public life and public discourse, and to root it out of the minds of the Soviet people.

The policy of the Soviet government toward religion was laid down in the first law on the subject in January, 1918. It was called "On the Separation of the Church from the State and of the School from the Church." To American ears, the title sounds harmless enough, but when the Soviets say "separation" they really mean it! In principle, the state will give not the slightest support whatsoever to the Church, and the Church is forbidden to engage in activities which are within the sphere of responsibilities of the state. This has a special meaning in a socialist planned economy of the Soviet type. It means, for example, that state publishing houses will not produce religious literature, and that churches may not give to the poor or carry on education. Moreover, schools are not merely to avoid the teaching of religion; they are actively to promote the teaching of atheism. These doctrines were spelled out in a 1929 law that remains the basic legislation on the subject to this day. There is freedom of religious worship, but churches are forbidden to give any material aid to their members or charity of any kind, or to hold any special meetings for children, youth, or women, or general meetings for religious study, recreation, or any similar purpose, or to open libraries or to keep any books other than those necessary for the performance of worship services. The formula of the 1929 law is repeated in the 1936 Constitution and again in the 1977 Constitution: freedom of religious worship and freedom of atheist propaganda—meaning (1) no freedom of religious teaching outside of the worship service itself, plus (2) a vigorous campaign in the schools, in the press, and in special meetings organized by atheist agitators, to convince people of the folly of religious beliefs.

The Criminal Code of the Russian Republic imposes a fine for violating laws of separation of the church from the state and of the school from the church, and, for repeated violations, deprivation of freedom up to three years (Article 142). Such violations include organizing religious assemblies and processions, organizing religious instruction for minors, and preparing written materials calling for such activities. Other types of religious activities are subject to more severe sanctions: thus leaders and active participants in religious groups that cause damage to the health of citizens or violate personal rights, or that try to persuade citizens not to participate in social activities or to perform duties of citizenship, or that draw minors into such a group are punishable by deprivation of freedom of up to five years (Article 227). This provision is directed primarily against Evangelical Baptists, Jehovah's Witnesses, Pentecostals, and other sects whose activities—though illegal—are quite widespread in the Soviet Union.

These laws were enacted as part of the severe antireligious campaign of Khrushchev in the early 1960s, when an estimated 10,000 Russian Orthodox churches—half the total number—were closed, together with five of the eight institutions for training priests, and the independence of the priesthood was curtailed both nationally and locally. (I speak of the Russian Orthodox Church, which is by far the largest, but the attack was on all religious communities.) This campaign ended with Brezhnev's accession to power in 1964; nevertheless, the rights of believers that were taken away in the Khrushchev period were not restored. The closed churches, monasteries, and seminaries remain closed. Parents who baptize their children must register, and may then be subject to harassment. Practical impediments are placed in the way of church weddings. Sermons are strictly controlled. Since 1959 or 1960 the Soviet leadership has returned to the policy which was criticized in the 1920s by the first Soviet Commissar of Education, Lunacharsky, who said, "Religion is like a nail—the harder you hit it on the head, the deeper it goes into the wood."

Despite this massive effort to suppress traditional religious belief, or perhaps partly because of it, there has been a strengthening of Christian faith. Christianity has not only survived the assault upon it but has been purged and purified by it.

What accounts for the extraordinary vitality of religious faith in the Soviet Union? The vitality of the Russian religious faith must be seen in the context of an atheistic Communist Party of 17 million members which has a virtual monopoly on high governmental and administrative posts. Members who are caught attending church services are subject to expulsion from the Party. Nor can we overlook the fact that the great majority of the youth, though by no means all, are atheists—45 million of them in the two Communist youth organizations, the Komsomol and the Pioneers, which, like the Party, are sworn to atheism. But the striking fact is that despite Soviet official claims to the contrary, and despite the superficial impressions of Western tourists, religion is not dying out in Russia. And it is not only the aged who cling to the church. It is possible, and even likely, that at least among the Russian half of the Soviet population, a majority of the adults are Christian. Also in the past decade there has been a substantial turn to Christianity among students and other young people. Soviet writers themselves have recently estimated the number of believers at twenty percent of the total Soviet population—about 50 million. Competent non-Soviet observers have said forty percent or more.

These are only guesses, since there are no published statistics. Also, there is no satisfactory definition of a "believer" (which is the word generally used in the Soviet Union for one who believes in God). I remember asking a Moscow taxi driver who was pointing out churches to me as we drove along whether he was a believer. He said, "No." I then asked him, "Do you ever go to church?" He answered, "No." I asked, "Never?" He replied, "Well, sometimes when things get very hard I go."

The evidence is strong, even without statistics, that, as a Russian Church leader said to me in Moscow, "Our people is a believing people, despite Communism."

Certainly, millions of Russians attend church services. I recall a Whitsunday service at the great Trinity Cathedral in Leningrad, where some 12,000 people stood for four hours in rapt devotion, packed together so there was hardly room to breathe. At another Leningrad cathedral every Wednesday night 4,000 people sing a special two-hour service; there is no choir, but the people know the words and music by heart. At a smaller church in Moscow on Easter eve my family and I arrived at 11:30 to find thousands already worshipping, and when we left at almost 4 a.m. we were among the first to go, while there were still people outside the church who had come too late to get in. Of course these large congregations result from the paucity of "working churches" (as they are called) that have been allowed to remain open. On the other hand, for every worshipper there are many more who would attend but for the political pressure not to.

What draws these people to the churches, six decades

after the Revolution made it very inconvenient, to say the least, to be religious? Partly, it is the experience of the Russian Orthodox liturgy which has a dramatic appeal of extraordinary power. The music carries you into another world. Time stands still. One's heart soars as the priest, the deacons, and the choirs sing prayers of praise, thanksgiving, suffering, penitence, forgiveness, and grace. The faces of the worshippers shine with devotion. The eyes of the priest burn with passion. The triumphant beauty of the singing is matched by the splendor and pathos of the icons. The priest and four or five deacons in resplendent robes of gold, green, blue, and white march in and out of the bema, carrying the Bible, chanting and enacting the drama of the liturgy.

Yet this is not merely an esthetic experience. Once when I was looking up at the icons on the ceiling of a church in Kiev, a young man behind me tapped my shoulder and said, "You are disturbing the worship; this is not a museum!"

The appeal of the Orthodox Church to the Russian is that it offers an answer to his deepest need, the need for an alternative to the hatred, sin, and violence of this world; indeed, an alternative to this world itself; his need to find a connection with other worlds, so that suffering and death will have a positive meaning.

The liturgy is the principal source of spiritual vitality in the Russian Church; the worship service, including the sacraments, is the heart and soul of Russian religious life. Deprived of religious education, of religious literature, of social activities of all kinds, the Russian Church has drawn its sustenance primarily from the liturgy, whose power has overcome the assaults of atheist propaganda in the minds of tens of millions of Soviet citizens.

The liturgy is, of course, more than mere ritual. It is the story of the Old and New Testaments and of the lives of the saints. It binds believers together in faith, hope, and love. The liturgy also includes the sermon, the word of the priest to his flock. The thirty or forty sermons which I have heard preached during fourteen visits to the Soviet Union in the past twenty-five years (including a twelve-month stay in 1961-62) stressed a few closely related themes: love of all men, forgiveness of enemies, unity of all people, joy in suffering.

Each sermon was based on a biblical text, usually a parable or an episode in Jesus' life. The priest would interpret the words of the Gospel and explain their deeper meaning. His message was essentially pastoral, delivered freely without notes, spoken with simplicity but without condescension, usually in beautiful, dignified biblical language which contrasted sharply with the stereotyped slogans of Soviet political speech.

"The kingdom of heaven is within us," one priest told his people. "It consists of love—not just love, but merciful love, inner peace with our neighbor and our enemy. It is said that this is unrealistic, that in fact man struggles to kill his enemy, and it is true that from generation to generation man has behaved that way. But the wickedness of man has not been able to destroy love, which still exists and which man is capable of realizing. But men cannot live a life of merciful love without suffering. That is the meaning of the cross. Christ showed us that through suffering we can manifest merciful love."

"It is a Christian's duty *not* to return evil for evil," said another priest at a church in Moscow which has the wonderful name Church of Joy of All Who Mourn. "We must hate the sin but not the sinner. Though Christians are scorned and offended, they return love. We rejoice in our suffering when we are scorned for Christ's sake—that is the meaning of the name of this Church, Joy of All Who Mourn."

"The most important expression of love for fellow-man," said another priest, "is love of homeland—for this means love of our brothers and sisters. Through love of homeland the whole earth can be united in love. All nations are equal in the sight of God."

There are many limitations upon what a Soviet priest can say in a sermon. He is not free to give concrete contemporary examples of the enemies to be loved; he is not free to criticize existing Soviet institutions or policies. Anything which can be called politics is excluded. But there is no doubt in the minds of his hearers of the implications of his words. And the next day his sermon will be reported in detail by his hearers to their neighbors in the communal kitchens of the crowded apartment houses, or at work or elsewhere, and they will draw the implications.

I heard a priest in Leningrad tell his congregation the story of Joseph's interpretation of Pharaoh's dream of the seven fat cows eaten up by the seven lean cows. "We are now living through the lean years," he said, "but we are nourished by all the riches which the Church has accumulated during the past centuries."

These riches are denied, by and large, to Soviet school children, who are taught to scorn them and who have not the experience to appreciate them. But Soviet young people in their late teens and twenties begin to doubt what they have been taught, and in their thirties and forties Soviet men and women often return to the Church, especially if life has been hard for them.

What I have been describing so far is the elemental confrontation of two fundamental faiths, Christianity and atheism, a confrontation that has existed in the Soviet Union for over sixty years. One is a faith in man's power to raise himself, by his own collective will and by disciplined obedience to the Communist Party leadership, to a political order of power and wealth and ultimately to a utopian social order of universal peace and brotherhood. The other is a faith in God's merciful forgiveness of human weakness and selfishness and in His offer of redemption from suffering and death to all who follow the example of Jesus Christ. Both these faiths have shown an extraordinary capacity to survive in the Soviet Union, despite frequent betrayal by their adherents.

That confrontation has, however, reached a new stage in the past twenty years, as many Christians, both individually and in small groups, have defied the Soviet state to live up to its own laws and its own professions of legality—those very laws and that very legality which repress religious activities, but which also offer some protections to freedom of religious worship.

The current struggle for more freedom of worship, and for more freedom to teach religion and to witness to religious faith outside the worship service, is linked with the struggle for legality, and has become increasingly important in the past twenty-five years. The very legal system which the Soviet state has used to contain and subdue religion is now being used by believers as a shield against those who would deprive them of those opportunities to which they are legally entitled.

In the late 1950s and early 1960s, Nikita Khrushchev raised the banner of socialist legality against the past excesses of Stalin's "cult of [his own] personality." This was a period of substantial law reform—which has continued, incidentally, under Leonid Brezhnev. The Stalin terror ended. The KGB itself was subjected to law.

Yet at the same time Khrushchev, starting in 1960, launched a systematic attack on religious belief in which basic principles of Soviet legality were violated. New *unpublished* laws and regulations were adopted—in violation, first, of the new legal requirements concerning publication of laws, and, second, of the fundamental principle of separation of church and state. Under these new unpublished laws the priesthood at the parish level was subjected to agencies of lay control within the church, and political pressures were exerted on those agencies of lay control to close churches, to require registration of baptisms, to divert to the state some of the money derived from contributions of the faithful, and the like. This was true primarily of the Russian Orthodox Church, although repressive measures were also taken against other permitted branches of Christianity (the "official" Baptists, the Lutherans, the Roman Catholics, and others) as well as against non-Christian religious faiths (Islam, Judaism), not to mention many sects that were banned altogether. Also laws confining religious rites to buildings authorized by the state to be houses of worship were invoked with increasing severity, and new religious communities were denied the right to build new houses of worship.

These and other repressions eventually bore unexpected fruit in the form of open opposition on the part of believers. This opposition was sometimes turned against those church leaders who had been co-opted to carry out the state's repressive measures, or who refused to speak out openly against them. Thus a number of independent clergy emerged, who demanded reform within the church itself. Others, both clerics and nonclerics, attacked Party and state policies and practices concerning religion, utilizing secret, though legal, channels to spread their views at home and abroad (so-called *samizdat*). Believers joined the growing number of "dissidents" who, starting mainly in the mid-1960s, risked prosecution for circulating anti-Soviet statements.

Such open opposition would have been impossible under Stalin; also it was more difficult under Khrushchev than it became under Brezhnev. It was connected with the increasing importance of legality in the Soviet Union. Especially after the death of Stalin, the strengthening of law and legality became essential to the Soviet leadership, both as a source of legitimacy and as a means of maintaining control of the Soviet people. At the same time, however, law and legality provided individuals and groups the opportunity to complain against abuses and to press for changes. As that freedom has increased, repressive measures and abuses of legality have also increased; yet the amount of liberalization has increased at a significantly more rapid rate than the amount of repression or abuse. Today there is a genuine ferment beneath the surface of Soviet life, an important part of which is manifested in the demand for further law reform and for stricter observance by the state of its own laws. Included among these laws are those protecting religious worship, making it a crime, for example, to interfere with lawful religious worship, or to discriminate in employment on the basis of religious belief.

Also it is permitted by Soviet law to teach religion to one's children. Yet in 1965 the then President of the Criminal Division of the USSR Supreme Court, G. Z. Anashkin, in an important article, found it necessary to criticize certain lower courts and administrative officials for punishing persons for educating their children in a religious spirit, which he said "does not constitute a crime," but on the contrary is protected by the constitutional freedom of worship. Judge Anashkin's reasoning gives an important clue to the sources of Soviet antireligious policy: administrative pressure against churches, he stated, "does not serve the struggle against the vestiges of religion. On the contrary, it reinforces religious fanaticism." Moreover, he stated, "It must always be remembered that every unjust or unjustifiably severe sentence can lead only to . . . the embitterment of the religious, and to consolidating and even intensifying their religious prejudices." He added that "The practice of exiling certain sects to other parts of the country . . . sometimes has the consequence that they become propagators of their 'teachings' in new places . . . [and] even . . . recruit individuals among the permanent population into their sects."

One is reminded again of Lunacharsky's analogy between the attack on religion and the hammering of a nail. "The harder you hit it, the deeper it goes into the wood."

Unfortunately, Judge Anashkin's strictures in 1965 did not prevent administrative and even judicial violations from continuing to occur. Such abuses were sometimes based on a provision of the 1968 Family Code that parents have a "duty" to raise their children "in the spirit of the Moral Code of the Builder of Communism." This Moral Code was interpreted to include the Leninist spirit of atheism, and was used especially against those radical sectarians who on religious grounds kept their children out of various school and social activities. In 1979 the Family Code was amended to eliminate this reference to the Moral Code of the Builder of Communism. The provision now reads: "Parents are obligated to bring up their children, care for their physical development and education, prepare them for socially useful work, and raise worthy citizens of the socialist society." This change reaffirms the principles which Judge Anashkin had espoused. It remains to be seen how it will be interpreted.

In reviewing a recent book by Michael Bordeaux and Michael Rowe, John Lawrence has written that "Soviet law is weighted against religious belief of all kinds, but, far worse, those limited rights accorded to believers in theory are denied them in practice. What the believers demand above all is that the law should actually be applied to them." Of particular significance in that statement, in my opinion, is the word "demand." What is new in Soviet Russia during the past fifteen years is that believers now do "demand" their rights under Soviet law, and that one of those rights is precisely the right to make such demands. Unfortunately, that right, too, is sometimes violated, with the result that the Soviet labor colonies now contain such prisoners as Kovalev, Ogorodnikov, Orlov, and other martyrs to their faith whose offense was that they protested too openly and too strongly against the violation of rights of believers. Yet for every person who is arrested, a dozen others rise up to protest.

The struggle for religious freedom—both freedom of worship and the opportunity to bear witness to religious beliefs outside the worship service—is linked with the struggle for legality in a deeper sense, as well. In the West a deep inner connection between law and religion has existed for 900 years. In Russian and Soviet history, law has not played so crucial a role either in political life or in religious life. Traditionally, the Russian Church has been an other-worldly church, and has tended toward antinomianism. Only in recent times has the inner link between religious freedom and legality become apparent to Soviet believers.

A Russian Orthodox priest, Father Dudko, who has been in great difficulty with both Church and Party authorities, recently told of a nine-year-old girl who came to confess her sins. He told her that she was too young to require confession. She then said she had a question. She had been told by her teacher, her classmates, and eventually her parents that she should join the Pioneers, which she did not want to do, because its credo includes opposition to religion. Under pressure, she finally joined, but then she secretly blessed her red Pioneer scarf with holy water. She wanted to know if that was wrong.

I believe this story is a paradigm of the present relationship of Christianity to the Communist Party in the Soviet Union. It is in many ways a paradigm of the relationship of religious faith to legal institutions in the United States as well.

If Christianity in the Soviet Union becomes allied with the struggle for legality, it is conceivable that someday the two together may help to soften the harshness of the Communist system, and to reform it in the direction of greater humaneness. It may be that something like this was in the mind of a lay leader of the Russian Church, whom I asked,

"What shall I tell Americans about the Russian Church?" He replied, "Tell them to get down on their knees and thank God for the Russian Church."

It is also conceivable that someday the two together—Christianity and respect for legality—may help to overcome the pervasive corruption of Communist society—the widespread bribery, black-marketeering, stealing of state property, drunkenness, and improper use of "influence" (*blat*)—which neither law alone nor law and scientific materialism together can overcome. For the inner connection between law and faith is much stronger than either Russian Christianity or Soviet Communism has yet realized.

My last point has to do with what we can learn from Soviet experience. We can learn to have a certain respect for militant atheism. The devil is no slob. There is a story of a little old lady who could never speak ill of anyone. She was asked what she thought of the devil. She hesitated, and then replied, "Well, he's very hard-working." She could have added that he is very intelligent, that he challenges us where we are most vulnerable. In Christian theology he is a fallen angel. What makes him the devil, as the late Bishop Emrich once said, is not that he lacks virtues, but that he is going in the wrong direction.

We are told that the devil tempted Christ with bread, with power over all the kingdoms of the world, and with miracles. So Soviet scientific materialism offers its adherents economic security, political power, and sensational technological progress—all in return for one thing: absolute subservience to the high priests of these gods, the Party. The challenge of this system *at home* is not that it will fail but that it will succeed—that it will meet its economic, political, and technological ends by means of the very discipline that it demands. For it is a system that, above all, by its means, meets certain real needs of twentieth century man—the need for unity and the need for a common social purpose.

The challenge *to us* is not only in the means but also in the ends. To make it our main purpose to accomplish those ends, but by a different means, is to fall into the danger of trying to serve both Mammon and God. Religion then becomes *our* means for accomplishing the wrong ends.

The Soviets believe what Jesus taught—that no man can serve two masters—no man can be a servant to both God and Mammon. So they have attempted to eliminate the belief in God. We, on the other hand, try to serve both God *and* Mammon, equally. Indeed, sometimes we think they are one. This *is* where we are most vulnerable.

The challenge, then, is obvious: we must construct a social order in which the goals of justice, mercy, and good faith—what Jesus called "the weightier matters of the law"—will take precedence over economic security, political power, and technological progress, and we must freely, through voluntary associations, pour into that social order the same spirit of service, self-sacrifice, and common purpose that under the Soviet system is induced by Party discipline.

10 PERSECUTION AND THE DEFENSE OF SPIRITUAL VALUES

Georgi Vins

Jesus said, "I am the way, the truth, and the life" (John 14:6). How is it that a person comes to know the Savior, Jesus Christ, under conditions of persecution and state atheism? God and God's truth are more powerful than atheism and Jesus Christ touched not only my heart, but the hearts of many people, many of my contemporaries.

I was born in 1928. I studied in Soviet schools where we were taught that there is no God. While I was growing up the opportunity still existed for Christians to study in universities and technical institutes. I finished my education as an electrical engineer at the Kiev Polytechnical Institute. (Many Christians of my generation were able to complete higher education.) We rejected the so-called truth that atheism offered us and found that Jesus Christ was the Truth. And we found that the life which Jesus Christ alone gives is real life.

We didn't start rejecting our government. We fulfilled our obligations as citizens by working, paying taxes and by doing other things required of citizens, but in the question of faith we said, "First place goes to Jesus Christ." We said that we would examine Soviet laws in the light of the gospel. Those laws which were acceptable, which did not contradict the Word of God, we fulfilled. But we would reject those that were not in accord with God's Word. We determined that the Bible is the absolute authority in all questions of life and faith. That's something that atheists didn't like. They believed that they should have control over everything—all questions of faith, all concerns of a man's soul. And that's where the conflict began. But we decided that we should listen to God, to obey God rather than man. That's what my generation began to do in the early sixties. And we knew that Jesus Christ was supporting us in that.

For the past twenty years a spiritual awakening, a revival, has been taking place in the Soviet Union. I know most about the life of Evangelical Christian Baptists in the Soviet Union, but there are believers of other denominations who love Jesus Christ, and many of them are also suffering for Jesus Christ in prisons and concentration camps. Today there are about 300 Christians incarcerated in Soviet prisons and concentration camps for their faith. This includes Orthodox believers, Lutherans, Catholics, Pentecostals and Adventists, as well as the Evangelical Christian Baptists. The percentage of Baptists in prison is very high. Of the 300 believers who are in prison for their faith, about 100 are Baptists.

Russia is traditionally a Christian country and the first baptism took place in the Orthodox Church about 1,000 years ago. The people at that time did not have access to the Bible. Halfway through the 1800s the Bible was translated into the Russian language and the simple folk began to read it. Until then it had been only in the ancient Slavonic language. In the middle of the last century the Evangelical Christian Baptist movement began and in 1867 the first Baptist believer was baptized. The revolution came about fifty years later in 1917. Forty of those fifty years were times of great persecution under the Czar and about ten years were in relative freedom. The revolution in 1917 was followed by another ten years of relative freedom because the new Soviet government had many other things to worry about and was more concerned with politics than religion.

But in 1929 a period of terrible persecution began. The legislation of 1929 regarding religious cults was passed. One point of that legislation states that any religious society must be registered with the government. That means that any fellowship or local church has to receive registration from the government in order to function. One of the demands is that no charitable work is allowed—no helping of needy people within the church. The church cannot collect offerings to help poor people. It is forbidden to have meetings for children, for women or for young people. Group Bible studies are prohibited. Christian literature discussion groups are forbidden. Christian excursions are forbidden. Christian children cannot gather even for recreation. It is forbidden to form a Christian library, to provide medical service among Christians, to help old or needy people.

Apparently the legislation wasn't enough. The atheists began an open warfare against the church and beginning in 1929 many pastors were imprisoned for their faith. Between 1929 and 1940, 25,000 Baptist pastors and ministers were arrested. Twenty-two thousand of those pastors died in concentration camps or prisons. Tens of thousands of Orthodox priests and ministers of the Lutheran Church, Pentecostal Church, and Catholic Church were also arrested. The church was not destroyed, though the persecution during Stalin's time was very terrible. We know what our Lord Jesus Christ said: "I will build my church, and the gates of hell will not prevail against it."

During World War II the anti-religious campaign

stopped to some extent and the church became very active. But it's interesting to note that the authorities wanted to gain control of the churches. In the early sixties the government began appointing those people who had contact with the government to high posts in the church. Men who stood for the independence of the church were not allowed in positions of leadership. The church didn't realize what was happening until the official center, the All-Union Council of Evangelical Christian Baptists (AU-CECB), put out a special letter of instruction that imposed limitations on the churches. This meant that not only were limitations imposed by the government, but also by ministers who had begun to compromise their faith.

Children were not allowed in churches. Sunday School and children's work were forbidden. Baptism for those under the age of thirty was forbidden. And there were many other limitations. But at the same time the limitations created a spiritual awakening—a revival—within the church. Exactly the opposite from what the atheists wanted was happening.

Even lukewarm Christians began to understand that when children were forbidden to come, the future of the church was being taken from them. That's when the independent churches began to form. Then these independent churches united. And today the independent Evangelical Christian Baptist union embraces approximately 2,000 churches across the country and includes more than 100,000 adult members.

The government then began its attack on that new church and many of the activists were put into prison. But that didn't stop the active church life. People began to love Jesus Christ more and to value the Bible more.

During the past twenty years from within the independent churches of the Soviet Union, three organizations have emerged: the Council of Evangelical Baptist

Churches, embracing 2,000 churches, the Christian Publishing House, and the Council of Prisoners' Relatives. All are unrecognized by the government, although not actually forbidden in the Constitution. The ministry of the Council is widespread evangelization within the country, the uniting of Evangelical Christian Baptists and fundamental believers within the country, and complete independence from the atheistic government.

Some of the key leaders of the revival in the Soviet Union have been persecuted and imprisoned. The KGB is now searching for Gennady Kryuchkov, the president of the Council of Evangelical Baptist Churches. They believe that if they can arrest him it will paralyze the church. Gennady Kryuchkov is living in hiding and carrying on his ministry in secret. He is a real activist for the independence of the church. In a recent letter Pastor Kryuchkov had some interesting comments on II Corinthians 10:4-5, which refers to our spiritual weapons. He said our weapons are intangible and unseen and cannot be destroyed. They can be passed across borders without hindrance. The KGB and atheists cannot take these weapons from us because these weapons are prayer, faith and God's Word.

It's wonderful to see that this man who has been so persecuted, now living and working in hiding, has such great faith, such faithfulness to God. Pastor Kryuchkov isn't alone. There are many courageous and faithful servants of God.

Another pastor, Nikolai Baturin, has been serving as General Secretary of the Council of Evangelical Baptist Churches, the capacity in which I served before I was exiled. He has been imprisoned a total of seventeen years for his active ministry and he is in prison again today— sentenced to five years hard labor. When Nikolai Baturin was a boy his father, also a Baptist pastor, was arrested and died in prison. Pastor Baturin has six children who are serving the Lord, witnessing to people around them of Jesus Christ.

Another pastor, Dmitri Minyakov, now sixty years old and imprisoned several times for his faith, is now in an Estonian prison. His health is in critical condition. A month before he was arrested I received a letter from him in which he said, "We will stand in truth as long as God gives us life. Our only desire is to remain faithful to Jesus Christ."

Where do they get such strength? It's the strength, the power of Jesus Christ. At one time Jesus asked his disciples, "Who do people think that I am?" And Peter answered, "You are Jesus Christ, Son of the living God." Jesus Christ said that on that confession of faith He would build His church and the gates of hell would not prevail against it.

The believers in my country are fundamental believers. We believe in Jesus Christ as the Son of God, in the teachings of Jesus Christ, in the whole Bible. We don't criticize the Bible. If we had liberal views about God's Word, we would have long ago been destroyed by atheism. We wouldn't have the strength, the power to withstand all the attacks. These views aren't just those of pastors who have been serving a long time, but also of many young people. Recently several young persons were arrested and tried for religious activities. Their "crime" was taking part in printing Bibles. At the trial one of the young women, Luba Kosachevich, proclaimed: "I love life. I love the blue sky. I love the flowers. But more than life I love Jesus Christ. And I will give my life to serve Him." Luba Kosachevich could have been released. All she had to do was deny Jesus Christ. But love for Jesus Christ is even stronger than the desire for freedom. Over the past twenty years a whole new generation of young people, born into a country of atheism, has come to love

Jesus Christ. The authorities did not want this to happen, but Christians began to defend the young people and children and we have a youthful church today. Young people, age 15-30, comprise approximately fifty percent of our membership. These are active young people who want to speak out for God.

But such activities are forbidden in our country. Preaching is permitted only in the church building. On one day 110 believers were baptized, and most of them were young people. About 1,500 people gathered at the river and the KGB was there, but was afraid to touch such a great number of people.

There is a great interest in God's Word among young people and among students too. The Russian people are tired of atheism, of godlessness. Not only the Russian people, but other national groups living in the Soviet Union are searching for Bibles. It is not possible to get a Bible in the library, or in a book store. Occasionally, the government allows a small edition of the Bible to be printed, but very few of these actually go to believers. Most of them are given to atheistic lecturers or sent out of the country. In Belgium one can buy Russian Bibles that have been printed in the Soviet Union. The Soviet government likes to give the impression that there are so many Bibles in the country that they can sell them in the West. In their thirst for God's Word many people copy the whole Bible by hand, and it ends up to be quite a few volumes. Others copy only the Gospels.

For five years after I became a Christian, I couldn't obtain a Bible. Finally I was able to buy a Bible for a whole month's wages. In the 1960s, at the beginning of the revival the Baptists decided it was necessary to have our own publishing house, a network of secret printing presses to print Bibles. All printing presses in the Soviet Union belong to the government, and we didn't want to be deceitful toward our government in the sense of stealing presses from them, because we knew that the gospel would not allow it. We prayed and worked hard in order to design and build our own printing presses, and the Lord blessed our work. In 1968 our offset printing press put out the first New Testament. It's a very simple machine, and it can be disassembled into several pieces, put into suitcases and carried from city to city across the country. Some of its components are taken from bicycles and motorcycles. The motor is from a washing machine. On this type of printing press, over the past twelve years, we have been able to produce over 500,000 pieces of literature, including Bibles and New Testaments.

We don't sell the books that we print. Everything is distributed free of charge. The price has already been paid—sometimes with lives. Others have paid with their freedom. There are people in prison today because they were printing Bibles. Small portions of the Bible, such as the Gospel of Mark, are also printed. This is a special edition for prisoners—so small that it can be hidden and read secretly. Bibles are forbidden in prisons and concentration camps. While I was in prison I had a Gospel of Mark that I read secretly and also shared with other prisoners.

Bibles printed secretly in the Soviet Union by independent Baptists are distributed free of charge throughout the country to people of all denominations. We share them with the Orthodox believers, with Pentecostal believers, with Lutherans, Catholics and people of other faiths, as well as with nonbelievers.

On the secret presses literature is printed not only in the Russian language but also in Moldavian and White Russian, in German for the Germans living in the Soviet Union, in Ukrainian, and in some minority languages for the people living in the far east of Russia. The independent Evangelical Christian Baptists are very missionary-minded, believing it is their responsibility to take the gospel to all the people in our country. For that reason we are cruelly persecuted. Of the 300 believers who are in prison today, 100 are independent Baptists.

The Christians in the Soviet Union deeply love their people; they would do anything for a spiritual awakening in our country. Russian people have a very special soul. They are kind, friendly people. But the atheists are carrying on a war against God. The atheists want to control the souls of the Russian people and all the people within the country, to rob us of our spiritual values. And they can't give anything in return.

Atheists have been in power in the Soviet Union for about sixty-three years. It would seem, according to atheist doctrine, that the church should be dead. But we see that exactly the opposite is happening. The people are being drawn to God and to Jesus Christ. That's the power of our Lord. It's not something that we've done, but because Jesus Christ today is as powerful and as mighty as ever.

The government also tries to manipulate and use official representatives of the church in a way that affects believers around the world. When the government realized the church couldn't be destroyed from the outside or by imprisoning believers it decided to try from within by using pastors in international politics. It's interesting, for example, to see the influence of the AUCECB, the official Baptist church council, on the Baptist World Alliance. For many years the Baptist World Alliance was passing resolutions on behalf of persecuted Baptists within the Soviet Union. In 1933 the Baptist World Alliance appealed to President Roosevelt asking him to do something about the persecution of believers in the Soviet Union. In 1934 at the Alliance's fifth congress, there was a strong defense of the Baptists who were being persecuted. In 1939, in Atlanta, Georgia, the Baptist World Alliance spoke out strongly in defense of Baptists who were being persecuted in the

Soviet Union and even in 1959 the issue was raised. But in 1955 the Soviet government had begun to allow the official AUCECB Baptist leaders to go to the Baptist World Alliance congress. And from that time the Baptist World Alliance was silent about persecution, because official representatives of the registered Baptist churches were actually approved and sent by the KGB. The KGB does not want the West to know or talk about the persecution of Baptists in the Soviet Union. Be attentive. These official representatives from the Soviet churches will always say that there is complete freedom for the church in the Soviet Union. And that's not a coincidence. They are fulfilling the task that they were given to do.

Many believers, living in West Germany, who had in their own time been imprisoned in the Soviet Union for their faith, asked for permission to speak from the platform of the Baptist World Alliance, but their request was denied. Last year the fourteenth Baptist World Alliance congress was held in Toronto. And again the voice of the persecuted church was refused a hearing. But we know that wasn't by coincidence. This can be a great danger for believers here in the West because many people in the West are not aware of what Soviet KGB agents are doing in the guise of religion. Christians have to be aware that the attack on religion in the Soviet Union isn't just a local issue—it's affecting the whole world.

Although religious instruction of children is forbidden, we have to find ways to tell children about God. We have organized secret Sunday Schools across the country. Children love to go to those Bible classes, and to hear about God. The Evangelical Christian Baptists in the Soviet Union don't have seminaries or Bible colleges to prepare pastors and future workers, so training of workers must begin while they are children. Preparing future pastors and Christian workers takes many years. Children live at home and go to atheistic schools, but in their free time they study the Bible.

Love for God is so great that everything is given in sacrifice, often life itself, sometimes freedom, and even one's family.

"How does a Christian feel when he has been imprisoned for his faith? How is it that God comforts?" It's really hard to be separated for many years from family and church. But even in those conditions God sends a very real help and comfort. I was imprisoned a total of eight years, four of them in the far northeast of Siberia near the city of Yakutsk. In the winter the temperature dropped to 64 degrees below zero. But the Lord doesn't abandon His children. In fact, the Lord spread His influence, not only to the prisoners but also to the officers. Some of the officers who guarded me had never seen a Bible before and they asked me questions about it. I witnessed to one officer a lot, and as he became more interested, he listened to Christian radio broadcasts in the Russian language from South Korea. His ideas began to change and secretly, when we were alone, he would share his thoughts. He said, "I have nothing to say, no objection to the very convincing power of the Gospel."

Another officer had somehow gotten his hands on a Bible temporarily, and in his office he was copying parts on a typewriter. Many others were openly opposed to the Gospel. There was one officer who told me I would never be free again. I was sentenced to ten years. He said, "After you finish those ten years, we'll give you another ten. You'll never be free. While you're still alive, while you still have your health, why don't you deny God? Eventually you'll have to deny God, anyway, so why don't you do it while you're young instead of when you're old and weak?" And then he came to me, just like the tempter, and said, "Where's your God? Why doesn't God intervene for you? You didn't steal anything or kill anybody. What are you doing in a prison with criminals?" Then he said, "Probably, God doesn't love you."

My release was really sudden. I thought that I never would be free again. I was amazed. I couldn't understand why people in the West were so concerned about me. But apparently God had His plan. While I was in a prison in Novosibirsk, I was taken to a cell in the middle of the night. There were twenty prisoners in that cell. I could tell that they were upset about something. None was sleeping. Many were smoking and the air was really thick. The prisoners' first question was, "Why are you in prison?" I said, "I'm a Christian." They said, "In this cell there are only murderers. Whom did you kill?" I said, "I didn't kill anybody. I'm a Christian. All I did was preach the Gospel." Then they started pushing even further. They said, "We're not just ordinary murderers. We have all killed three, four, five men. So how are you going to prove you're a Christian? Do you have a Bible?" Bibles are forbidden in prisons in the Soviet Union and officers often search prisoners and confiscate what they find. But I had hidden away my Gospel of Mark, wrapped in some rags in my bag. I pulled it out and showed it to those murderers. They wouldn't take this Gospel into their hands. The Russian people have a special reverence, a high regard for the Bible, and these men knew that their hands had shed blood. They felt that they couldn't hold that Gospel in their hands. But I told them, "Take it. It was written for people to read." And I watched as these men held Scripture in their hands for the first time. I was really tired that night. For two days and two nights I hadn't slept, but there was no place for me to lie down. And then one of the prisoners said, "Here, take my cot." I immediately fell asleep.

When I awoke the next morning I noticed that nobody else had been sleeping. All of the prisoners were seated in a circle and one was reading the Gospel of Mark aloud. He had come to the last chapter. I noticed that they weren't smoking. There was a different expression on their faces; they seemed relaxed and even friendly. Then one of the prisoners said to me, "Can God forgive me? I have killed five men." And I told him, "God can forgive you. Jesus Christ forgave the thief hanging on the cross next to Him. He will forgive you if you repent, if you leave your criminal life."

I spent a week in that cell with those murderers. We spoke a lot about God. And then they asked me for my Gospel of Mark. Each one of them had a very long sentence ahead—at least fifteen years. They said, "Give us your Gospel of Mark." I didn't really want to give it up. It had been with me all the way through prison and I wanted to save it. I hoped that someday, when I was free, I would be able to give it to my children. But when these men asked for my Gospel, I gave it to them. I especially remember one prisoner who said, "God will send you many Bibles, many New Testaments." I didn't know what the future held for me, but ten days later I was in New York City. I do have many Bibles and New Testaments today. And when I was speaking in West Germany a young person there gave me a Gospel of Mark, just like the one I had given away.

My release from Soviet imprisonment came unexpectedly. I was taken to a prison in Moscow. The next day I was taken to a special room and the guards told me to undress and to put on a suit, a white shirt and a necktie that were lying on a table. In the Soviet Union all prisoners wear a very dark, simple uniform. I didn't know why they wanted me to change, but I had a feeling that they were going to show me to some American tourists, so they could see how well Soviet prisoners dress. But then they announced that I was being exiled from my country, that I was stripped of my Soviet citizenship and was being sent to the United States. They also said, "You are now the most unfortunate of all men. Nobody needs you. You are a man without a country." But then I thought, "Who can take my heavenly homeland from me? Who can take Jesus Christ from me?" I was sure that the Lord would be with me in America.

The brothers and sisters who are still in the Soviet Union appointed me to be the official representative of the independent Evangelical Christian Baptist church and we have opened a representative office in Indiana. Part of my task is to inform Christians in the West about the situation of believers in the Soviet Union. I maintain secret contacts with brothers in the Soviet Union and I try to use every opportunity to speak to Christians here in America. I have been to Europe five times and to Australia as well as speaking in the United States. My message to believers in the West is to value the freedom you have, love Jesus Christ, cherish the Bible. And make use of opportunities to witness.

Great dangers face America. Atheism is active here. It's just that atheism hasn't come into government power as it has in the Soviet Union. Many of the symptoms are present in America that were at one time visible in the Soviet Union. Now it's forbidden to pray in public schools and that began in the 1960s. In the same years that prayer was being forbidden in public schools in the United States, the law was being passed in the Soviet Union prohibiting children to enter a church building. But in America you still have churches and Christian schools. Nevertheless, the attack against the church has begun. I think there are great problems in the United States and one is that many are apathetic about Jesus Christ.

One of the things that upset me most when I came to America was widespread liberal views within the church. I have met pastors, even Baptist pastors, who do not believe in the deity of Jesus Christ. Some do not believe in the

Holy Bible. For that same Bible many believers are dying in Soviet prisons. Many others are working hard so that people in our country can have the Bible. The presence of liberal views is a very great danger for believers in America.

There is something I think that Christian attorneys can be doing that will help Christians in America, in the Soviet Union and around the world. I think it is important that they study the *Legislation on Religious Cults,* the legislation of 1929, which is a great evil in the Soviet Union, and bring this document to the attention of the American people. Perhaps Christian attorneys can also help those who are imprisoned in the Soviet Union for their faith. Many of the believers need a defense attorney. At first the Soviet Union probably will not allow lawyers from the West into the country, but it is important to start action in that direction so that every trial that takes place against Christians in the Soviet Union will be known by Christians in the West.

When I was tried in 1974 I requested a Christian lawyer, but in the Soviet Union they couldn't find one. So the message went out to the West for a Christian lawyer to defend me at my trial. Alf Haerem, a Norwegian attorney, was willing to come, but he wasn't allowed into the country. The fact that he wanted to defend me and appealed through official channels to come exerted a great pressure on the government and helped me. The accusations against me all involved religious activities: teaching children about God and teaching young people about God. Another charge was Psalm 23, because this psalm was discovered along with a commentary about that psalm in my handwriting when I was arrested. At my trial I said that actually the psalm was written by King David, so King David should be tried. I told the judge, "What you need is a Christian lawyer. You can't understand what this trial is all about unless you have a Christian lawyer to explain it to you."

So my appeal to Christian lawyers is to be ready, to be willing to go to the Soviet Union and defend those Christians who are being tried for their faith. It is important that Americans know that in the Soviet Union there are many Christians and they are praying for a spiritual awakening in America. They hope you pray for a spiritual awakening in the Soviet Union. May the name of our Lord Jesus Christ be glorified! Amen.

AFTERWORD

Julius B. Poppinga

"True justice is the first pillar of good government." I have reflected on these words which are inscribed above the Corinthian columns of the New York State Courts Building at Foley Square in New York City. Can there be any justice but true justice? Not in the philosophical sense, but certainly in the practical sense. The system of justice can be twisted. Good lawyers can make bad justice. Bad lawyers and bad judges can make it even worse. And bad justice makes for bad government. What is it that sets the course against that? It is the dynamic of the Holy Spirit who guides us into all truth and to true justice. We need to be open to this dynamic.

Christ's followers should be *the agents for justice*. We are admonished by the prophet Micah to do justice, love mercy, and to walk humbly with our God. Isaiah tells us that we are to seek justice, to relieve the oppressed, to judge the fatherless and to plead for the widow. It is very clear that when we speak of justice in the biblical sense we are not just talking about giving what is due. We are talking about meeting need wherever it exists, and particularly where it exists most helplessly.

As Christ's followers we are called to work for justice in an imperfect context, an imperfect society and through an imperfect system. The biblical concern for justice is clearly a call to action. Consider Micah's "Do justice, love mercy." Someone has observed that instead of doing justice and loving mercy we find it easier to *do* an occasional act of mercy and to *love* justice in the abstract. In fact, many of us don't love mercy at all. We love vengeance. We like the retribution that the letter of the law metes out. But we are to *love* mercy. And we are not only to talk about justice, but to *do* justice. That is the difficult part. The Lord's Prayer admonishes, "Thy will be *done*"—not debated, not meditated upon, not admired—but "*be done*" and "be done on *earth*"!

I am convinced that the lawyer, before he can begin to do justice, must seriously examine his attitudes. He has been schooled in a way which produces a machine, a technical expert, someone who stands aside from need and kind of works with it, but doesn't really get involved. If we look at the biblical example of justice as it is embodied in Jesus Christ, we see characteristics which challenge the lawyer's attitudes toward justice. We find that in order to do justice the *legitimacy of the emotions* must be recognized. In the feeding of the five thousand, the disciples saw the need but stopped short of compassion. "The people are hungry. Let's send them away so that they can get food," they said. But Jesus was moved with compassion and He said, "Feed them right here." We need to feel compassion so that we do not treat the need in an impersonal way but rather that our heart goes out toward that need.

This was demonstrated again when the people brought their little children to Jesus. The disciples saw this as an intrusion: they wanted the kids to go away, to leave the Master alone and to leave *them* alone. But we read that Jesus was moved with indignation. It is that kind of indignation that is legitimate, and it has to be present in those who would act effectively for justice.

Along with compassion and indignation, grief is a legitimate emotion that we must feel if we are to respond to the needs of justice. Again Jesus sets the example. After Lazarus had died Jesus came and found Martha and Mary and their friends weeping. And then we read that great favorite of all Sunday School children who have to memorize verses: "Jesus wept." He entered fully into their grief.

A further requisite, in addition to the element of emotion, is that of *identification,* which Jesus demonstrated to the full when He identified with us in death. I believe one reason Jesus wept when Mary and Martha were weeping was because He recognized that they too, His good friends, were under the oppression of sin and death, and He entered into that misery with them. Then more profoundly at the cross He entered into the experience of death—once and for all to gain victory over sin and death for all men.

To be added to emotion and identification is the need for *submission to the servant role.* This does not come easy for the attorney. He too often sees himself as the leader, the dominant personality. To empty himself, to have the servant mind of Christ, does not come naturally for the lawyer.

We do well to consider an observation made by Joseph A. Tetlow, writing in *America* magazine. In discussing the metaphor of the salt and the light, he writes, "To be the salt of the earth and the light of the world is not to belong to a nifty elite, risen sun-like above the herd. Any disciple caught preening himself over Christ's metaphors has seriously misunderstood them. We do not lie around being salty or shoot across the world like stars. The salt is poured out, spent. The lamp burns away, serving. Isaiah 58:7-8: 'Share your bread with the hungry, shelter the homeless poor. Clothe the man you see naked. Then will your light shine like the dawn.' "

ABOUT THE CONTRIBUTORS

William Ball is a partner with the Ball & Skelly law firm in Harrisburg, Pennsylvania. He received his A.B. degree from Western Reserve University in 1940 and his J.D. degree from the University of Notre Dame College of Law in 1948. His practice has involved him in cases in twenty states and the Supreme Court including *Wisconsin v. Yoder*, the case of Amish parental rights. He has lectured and debated on constitutional law at several universities. He is on the National Advisory Board for the Center for Law & Religious Freedom.

Professor Harold J. Berman is James Barr Ames professor of law at Harvard Law School. He received his J.D. degree from Yale Law School in 1947. He has written and lectured widely in the field of Soviet law, the law of international trade, and comparative legal history. His books include *Justice in the USSR* (second edition 1963), *The Interaction of Law and Religion* (1974), and *The Nature and Functions of Law* (fourth edition 1980).

Lynn R. Buzzard is executive director of the Christian Legal Society in Oak Park, Illinois, and also serves on the board of the Committee on Religion and Law in Boston, Massachusetts. He received his B.A., M.A.T., and M.Div. degrees from San Francisco Theological Seminary. He has also studied law at Notre Dame University School of Law. He has authored several books, including *Christian Perspectives on Law and Theology* and *Tell It to the Church: Reconciling Out of Court*.

Charles W. Colson, former special counsel to President Nixon, founded Prison Fellowship after serving a federal prison term for a Watergate-related offense. He is the author of two books, *Born Again* and *Life Sentence*. He is rapidly emerging as the chief spokesman for prison reform in America.

Dean M. Kelley has been director of religious and civil liberty at the National Council of Churches since 1960. He is a graduate of Denver University (A.B., 1946) and the Iliff School of Theology (Th.M., 1949). He is the author of *Why Conservative Churches Are Growing* (Harper & Row, 1972, 1977) and *Why Churches Should Not Pay Taxes* (Harper & Row, 1977). He is editing a book on government intervention in religious affairs, to be published by Pilgrim Press in 1982.

Dr. Joel Nederhood, director of The Back to God Hour ministries of the Christian Reformed Church, located in Palos Heights, Illinois, has been associated with this broadcasting outreach since 1960 and has served in his present capacity since October 1965. Christian Reformed broadcasting ministries now include radio broadcasts in English, Arabic, Spanish, Portuguese, French, Indonesian, Chinese, Japanese, Russian, and the work of CRC-TV, the television arm of the Chicagoland organization.

Dr. Nederhood is an ordained minister in the Christian Reformed Church. He holds a doctorate from the Free University of Amsterdam, and is also a graduate of Calvin College and Seminary in Grand Rapids, Michigan.

Julius B. Poppinga is a graduate of Wheaton College and the University of Michigan Law School where he served as associate editor of the Michigan Law Review. He is a member of the bar of the States of New York and New Jersey and is a member of the law firm of McCarter & English, with offices in Newark, New Jersey, and New York City. Mr. Poppinga served as chairman of the Church and State Committee of the American Bar Association's Section on Individual Rights and Responsibilities. In 1978 he was elected president of the Christian Legal Society for a four-year term. He is an elder in Grace Presbyterian Church, Montclair, New Jersey.

Dr. Francis A. Schaeffer is the author of twenty-three books which have been translated into twenty-five languages. His latest book is *A Christian Manifesto,* an urgent call for the West to return to its Judeo-Christian heritage. With his wife, Edith, the Schaeffers founded L'Abri Fellowship, an international study center and community in Switzerland. At present, there are branches of L'Abri in England, the Netherlands, Sweden, and the U.S.

Robert Toms is a partner with the firm of Caldwell & Toms in Los Angeles, California. He received his B.A. degree from Bob Jones University in 1957, and his J.D. degree from Duke University in 1965. He is a member of the North Carolina and California state bars. He is counsel for the Association of Christian Schools International, and is a former president of the Christian Legal Society.

Georgi Vins, a Russian Baptist pastor, was imprisoned in

Soviet concentration camps a total of eight years for his active ministry as secretary general of the Council of Evangelical Baptist Churches. Rev. Vins was stripped of his Soviet citizenship and exiled to the United States of America in April 1979 in a dramatic exchange of five prisoners for two captured Soviet spies. In the special agreement between U.S. President Jimmy Carter and Soviet President Leonid Brezhnev, Vins' family, consisting of his mother, wife, five children, and a niece, was allowed to join him in the West. Rev. Vins resides in Elkhart, Indiana, where he has established the International Representation for the Council of Evangelical Baptist Churches of the Soviet Union. Vins was appointed by the persecuted church in the Soviet Union to be their representative in the West. He travels widely, alerting Christians about the dangers of atheism and informing them regarding the true situation of Christians in his homeland. He maintains close contact with believers in the Soviet Union, and organizes aid to the persecuted church through secret channels. For more information regarding this ministry write: P.O. Box 1188, Elkhart, Indiana 46515.

Dr. Bernard Zylstra is professor of political and legal theory at the Institute for Christian Studies in Toronto, Canada. He received his B.D. degree from Calvin Theological Seminary in 1958, his LL.B. degree from the University of Michigan Law School in 1961, and his S.J.D. degree from the Free University of Amsterdam in 1968. His numerous writings include publications on Harold Laski, Karl Marx, Herman Dooyeweerd, Herbert Marcuse, George Grant, Eric Voegelin, and Daniel Bell. He also serves as principal of the Institute for Christian Studies.